THE ART OF FOCUS

10,9

THE ART OF FOCUS

10,9

CHRISTINA BENGTSSON

Reclaim Focus Academy

Cover & Design: Elsa Wohlfahrt Larsson
Translation: Stuart Tudball

Printed by CPI, Leck, Germany
First edition, first print

ISBN 9798742387503

Bio

"I am, however, humble enough to appreciate the impossibility of being able to teach other, already gifted, people to live in a new, focused and infallible way. No-one would ever be so bold, and infallible living is not the goal. It is simply a case of discovering the tiny difference between focused and unfocused, and what this little nuance in existence can mean"

Christina Bengtsson

About Christina

Christina Bengtsson, born and raised on the Swedish countryside, is an author, international speaker, military officer and precision shooting World Champion. With her exceptional background, international reach and acclaimed book "The Art of Focus – 10.9," Christina is considered a global thought leader on the topic of focus.

Christina has spent her whole career exploring focus – an essential skill in today's society with its intensive demands on performance – and its application to both our professional and personal lives. She has the tools to help us regain command of this crucial ability in both the short and long-term to live a more fulfilling, purposeful, and balanced life.

She is trained at the US Army Marksmanship Unit and has been recognized with the Swedish Supreme Commander's cion. Christina´s experience is an exceptionally useful teaching on one of today's most important topics to engender sustainable change with high results.

Today, she lectures and speak to audiences worldwide, from TEDx stages to international business schools and major corporations. The more people who learn about the value of a focused mindset, the healthier our world will be.

"From the individual to society at large, it's time to reclaim our focus".

Christina Bengtsson

Just one shot left. For the sixtieth time this morning, my shooting requires absolute stillness. There is a burning pain in my left arm and I can hear my pulse beating. In the screen of the results monitor beside me I can see the reflection of everyone who has left the grandstand to get a closer look as I fire my final shot. Their presence reminds me of my lead and the fact that my ultimate goal is within reach. A nine now will probably lose me the title. A mere millimetre at a distance of fifty metres could transform this potential triumph into yet another fiasco. With these irritatingly tight margins, the alarming thoughts running through my head and this racing pulse, the outcome might easily be an embarrassing seven. How much time is left in the match? I aim, hold my breath and stare intently through the sight. I can't let this opportunity slip away. The idea, despite a clear lack of sense and concentration, of just shooting and getting it all over with is tempting. If it ends badly, I can always blame the wind. Focus!

I decide to stop staring down the sight an interrupt my shot to get some focus. I lower my gun and rest both my arm and my mind. There is a murmur from the spectators. With the little time left in the match and only one shot left, I know they are wondering why I'm choosing to rest and break off a good shooting stance. Now, composed, conscious of my thoughts and of the seconds ticking away, I coolly take another few seconds of rest. "Don't shoot a seven..." and "what will coach say if I miss out on a medal again...?" are replaced with one simple thought about the lovely autumn leaf that is playing in the wind just ahead of me. The leaf has my full attention, my worries melt away and a sense of contentment flows through my body. I lift my gun and begin my last shot in this drama. Time ticks away. I wait another few seconds to be sure of myself. The wind has to be right, with the thought about the leaf dominating and keeping the other thoughts at bay. Not many seconds left. The spectators hold their breath and I enjoy the moment. There is tension in the air and a chilly calm prevails. If these seconds could last an eternity, I would choose to stay here forever…

Bang!

10.9 flashes up on the screen. I'm world champion.

TABLE OF CONTENTS

My Passion for Focus

As a child I was good at most sports. I thought running, particularly running really, really fast, was the best thing ever. Every morning I raced Hetty the horse to the school bus, which stopped on the main road, just beyond the end of the horse's paddock. By that time of my life, I had been running and jumping around so much that I was a muscular little tomboy with thighs that wouldn't have looked amiss on an ostrich. Since we had our own well at home on the farm, my blond hair had been discoloured by copper deposits and turned green. This combination earned me the nickname of The Hulk.

I made good use of the school's running track, not least when in fourth grade I was challenged to a race by long-legged Henrik in sixth grade. The day when friends and teachers came to watch the battle between Henrik the Tall and The Hulk is one of the strongest sporting memories of my life. It was hard to say who crossed the finishing line first, but it was clear that I was closing in more and more and looked like the victor in the race. I gave it everything I had and ran as if my life depended on it. Being surrounded by jubilant friends and cheering teachers was so encouraging and so life-affirming that there was no prouder person on the planet in that moment.

This may be the first time I got to experience the feeling of being a winner, if only for a day. A victory of this kind was a new experience, and one that I was completely bowled over by. Nothing could be better.

Haunted by this memory, 13 years later I found myself standing outside the student residences of Chalmers University of Technology in Gothenburg with my visiting parents. I had long felt I had some inner capability. It was like a kind of persistent energy that I didn't know what to do with. Being best at something was the only thing I could imagine might satisfy this inner drive, and now I had to tell my mother and father that I had decided to focus on one thing and be the best in the world at it. I guess it had to be in a sport. I was worried about how my parents would react to my decision. They had always guided me, helped me and supported me through thick and thin, but they had never really been great cheerleaders for sport. Going into sport was no safe bet in this life. But I was sure it was what I wanted, and I so wanted them to be as understanding about this choice as they had been about all the others.

After a bit of small talk, I announced in a determined voice: "Mum, Dad, I have to compete." My determination must have been irresistible. They looked at me and at each other, followed by a few seconds of hesitation, and then it was smiles all round. Their joy at knowing after upper secondary school their daughter had finally become enthused by something meant they welcomed what I told them with open arms. What a relief! I was filled with courage and with even more determination. My worries subsided and I felt a fantastic sense of liberation. Imagine knowing what I want to do, deciding to do it, and gaining the support of those closest to me. I was so happy.

However, I had not yet decided which sport to focus on. The following day my brother also became involved, and he suggested that I was perhaps already too old to be the world's best sprinter. Following a brief period of consideration, I opted for shooting, a sport that I knew about, and that I thought I could continue for quite a long time. And so began a new chapter in my life. I sourced the equipment I thought I needed and threw myself into training. It would take me three years of manic practice and mostly coming last before I could even hope to compete with other shooters in Sweden.

In the summer I competed almost every weekend. And every time I came last, I cried. I couldn't comprehend how it could be so damn difficult! After all, I was so committed, so strong-willed and so goal-oriented. Seeing my name at the bottom of the results table hurt the same every time. The thought that the others had been shooting since they were kids, compared with me who had just started, gained no traction with me. In my world, I was programmed to win, but I didn't. That made me feel so disappointed, so small and so sad. What had I let myself in for? What was this longing that I had succumbed too? Could I ever be happy in this new life?

Focused and alone, I travelled the land losing and losing.

But my conviction remained. After all the last places, dejection, doubt and tears came disciplined training.

And it was this determination that brought me into the military arena. It was a couple of years later when I randomly came across an ad by the Swedish Armed Forces seeking "an elite sportsman or woman with good leadership skills" and offering the opportunity to undergo officer training at the same time as being able to train and compete in sport. Now that I had the odd medal at district level, I decided that this position would be mine. I applied, was accepted and began my military service at the air force base F7 Såtenäs.

I trained early in the morning before formation and then late in the evening. To fit in three shooting sessions per day, whenever possible I also rushed off to the air rifle range at lunchtime. We weren't actually allowed to be in the shooting range after a certain time in the evenings, but I have to confess that with the help of my military service buddies, I smuggled in a mattress and spent the night inside. This proved a smart move, as it meant I could quickly get into early morning training and I would even train in the middle of the night as a way to practise my technique and balance at different times of the day. I was never found out.

In my first year as an officer at base F7, and later at the Military Academy, I practically lived at various shooting ranges and quickly developed into an established national shooting team member. My determination had begun to show in the results tables. The losses were mixed with successes, and I no longer felt like a lonely outsider in the shooting world. In stark contrast to the time when my schoolmates called me The Hulk, I was now a tall, slim, military markswoman with a mop of blonde hair and no hint of green. Instead of running and jumping, I now lay or stood stock still in exactly the same spot for five hours a day, focusing on a dot 50 metres away.

Over the many years that I improved my capacity for precision, I increasingly pondered over the true difference between my successes and my failures, and over the subsequent joy and frustration that constantly alternated within me. The early years were largely down to technique. At that time, keeping still, relaxation, recoil management and choice of ammunition determined whether or not I succeeded. But when, after a number of years, I broke through a barrier of technical frustration and achieved a necessary level of technical brilliance, the difference between successful and unsuccessful matches became more difficult to pin down. I travelled all over the world, and usually performed less well abroad than I did when training at home. In most cases, I could deliver world-class points the day before a championship, and then later in the crucial match I would completely unravel and fall far short of my actual capabilities. My thoughts and my emotional state had much more of an impact on my results than technique. I soon came to realise that this phenomenon affected the vast majority of my fellow shooters and competitors. This was a problem I needed to deal with, and so my interest in being able to control my thoughts became my passion.

During every training session, I now started to take notes not only on the weather, wind, light, diet, stretching, body stillness, target patterns and choice of sight ring, but also my thoughts, emotions and mindset before and after the training or the match. I gradually realised that the technical level of my shooting could always be fine-tuned, but that this was less critical than what I was thinking in the different situations.

I mapped out my thoughts, where they came from and what impact they had on both my emotional state and my end performance. I listened to my fellow shooters and monitored some of them closely. Once enough shots had been fired and enough thoughts noted down, I began to see a pattern. We all seemed to work in quite similar ways.

After years of taking notes that I initially categorised as "mental", I eventually narrowed my knowledge and insights down into the category of "focus". This very phenomenon appeared to be critical in so many situations, playing a role not only in high-pressure shooting finals but also in the longer, broader perspective and in everyday life.

But it was not just in my shooting that these ideas took hold.

As an officer in the Armed Forces, I was privileged to be part of FM Elit, a small group of top sportsmen and women who were able to combine their job and their sport. Half of the time at work was set aside for training and competing. The international competitions quickly ate up this time, so training early in the morning and late at night continued. But the combination of elite sport and a regular job was superb in that I was able to analyse the phenomenon of focus and apply my passion in a context other than the sporting world. It was not only in shooting finals that I faced pressure and challenges and benefited from my own theories, but also in my work in the military arena. As head of the International Military Sports Council's European office, a post I took on the same year I won my first World Championship title, I often trained under a pressure that was not unlike having all eyes on me as I stood in the final line-up on the shooting range. I saw the phenomenon everywhere, both professionally and privately, in both a short-term and a long-term perspective, and it´s great impact in people´s lives. Especially in this modern world where countless distractions compete for our attention. Following observations and analyses in several places around the world, in several different cultures and contexts, I was able to establish that the phenomenon and its importance are universal.

I had assumed that the conversations I was having with myself over the years were only of any use to me in my own development. But when I talked to other people and received a positive response to my reflections, I soon realised that others could also benefit, particularly those with their own drive and an appetite to learn new skills.

In the beginning, I took what I had observed and learned to be a natural process – a kind of "school of life" that I assumed everyone had attended. It was interesting to learn that few people, if any, receive the same schooling as oneself. Therefore every individual's experience is worth sharing with others, because of its uniqueness. In my case, I can guarantee that no-one has learned their life lessons the same way I have, and no-one else has nine volumes of hand-written thoughts from shooting ranges in different parts of the world. The motivation to put my reflections down in black and white and share them gradually grew as I reduced my own involvement in sport, and the desire to help other people improve became as strong a driver as the desire to stand alone on the podium with a medal around my neck. I am, however, humble enough to appreciate the impossibility of being able to teach other, already gifted, people to live in a new, focused and infallible way. No-one would ever be so bold, and infallible living is not the goal. Chasing after such a goal would mean losing yourself in the effort of achieving the impossible. It is simply a case of discovering the tiny difference between focused and unfocused, and what this little nuance in existence can mean. It is not about becoming something new, or something better, but simply about functioning exactly as good as we already are, and understanding that this is sufficient for both general happiness and great deeds.

That day outside the student residence at Chalmers, when I decided to focus on one thing and be the best at it, I also came up with a motto for myself, a kind of vision for my future:

In my case the push for gold is not only about striving for a medal around my neck, but also about striving for personal development.

My motto came to mean much more for my approach to my sport than I ever could have known on the day that I wrote it. At that time, I had no idea about the value of maintaining a distance from what I had chosen to invest my time and energy in achieving.

The motto reminded me that the value never lay in the actual medal. It made it clear to me that my work and my successes would be more enduring and more valuable when something other than the simple desire to win was the main driver. I probably already had a strong inner desire to learn and develop more than an ability to shoot sixty 10s in a row and be top of the podium. It was probably on that first day of my future life, when I wrote my motto, that my journey towards an interest in focus and concentration and developing this fascinating capacity began. I just didn't know it then. At the time, I simply wanted to compete, with the ultimate goal of becoming the best in the world. Training hard was the only practical way forward that I knew. The fact that, over my 15 years as a precision markswoman, I had a broader drive than winning medals gradually became clearer and clearer, particularly once my technical level had reached its peak and the psychological aspects of the matches became more critical. It was then that I also realised it was no longer the number of hours I put in, but the quality and focus of the training that put me a cut above the rest. Alongside all the notes I made, I began devouring books and research on this subject. A kind of new motto was never to travel to an international competition or training session without a book in my bag.

Everything came into sharp focus for me later on in my career. After countless losses, a World Championship gold and a number of other prestigious medals that I was extremely pleased to receive, I began to wonder about the subdued pleasure I took from my latest performances and new metals. Once home from Croatia, a medal in my bag, I talked to my close friend Mats about this feeling over a glass of water and some oat cakes (usually the only thing I had in after a long time away): "It feels as if I don't need any more medals..." Mats answered with absolute conviction: "Christina, for you shooting has only ever been a tool for your own personal development."

It was only later that I realised the significance of what Mats had said. He was right. The fact that he was right did not mean I had lost my competitive instinct or that I had reached some sort of state of comfortable satisfaction, but that I had a desire and need for further development. It was time for a new challenge.

I fired my last shot at the World Games on the newly built Olympic range in Rio de Janeiro. You might think that it was important for me to end on a high and achieve another world-class championship win, and last but not least go out with a perfectly centred 10.9 on my final shot. But no, that wasn't the case – I ended up missing out on the final by a wide margin, and in my final round I shot two 9s to the left. An icy feeling of shame quickly spread through my body, but it was outweighed by the joy I then felt after my very last shot. It was overwhelming. I beamed as if I had beaten the world record, and absurdly the photographers rushed towards me in the belief that they were capturing the smile of a champion. In actual fact, it was the happiness of a loser now able to focus fully on a great new challenge that was drawing the attention of the camera lenses. It was the same happiness I felt that day, 15 years earlier, when I decided to be the best in the world at one thing. With that goal achieved, it was time to move on to the new task of helping the world with the art of focus.

I have written this book to give a clear picture of what focus is, how important it is and how it can be achieved. The book explains what in life affects our focus, as regards individual feats and in our search for a generally satisfying life.

It can be confusing with all different expressions regarding focus; short-term focus, long-term focus, concentration, attention etc. To clarify, the psychology separates out five different types of concentration under the umbrella term of "attention": selective attention, which is the capacity to filter out any distractions from what you have chosen to focus on; alternating attention, which is the capacity to intentionally switch between different tasks; sustained attention, which is the capacity to maintain a focus on something for a prolonged period; divided attention, which is what we generally call multitasking; and focused attention, which is about homing in one specific thing.

In the book I use focus as an umbrella term for all the different types.

To somehow illustrate the difference between focus and concentration, see concentration as a condition for achieving and maintaining focus. A shooter who concentrates on every shot, on all the training sessions throughout the year, and then sixty times in a row in competition, will retain focus all through the match. If you concentrate on everything you commit to, you will also find it easier to stay on track, do the right thing and steer yourself towards a life in focus.

⚜ ⚜ ⚜

Throughout the book we will learn about sharp focus and relaxed focus as well as automatic focus and controlled focus.

All the chapters in the book take their inspiration from shooting. It is around the shooter's precision, stamina and endless practice at winning and losing that the ideas have crystallised. However, I will show how the benefits of focus reach far beyond the shooting ranges and how much more there is to focus than meets the eye.

It is about selecting the right thoughts from the thousands in your head – ignore what´s irrelevant and doing one thing at a time and doing it well.

Staying sharp under pressure and being yourself.

Daring to make a choice and stick with that choice when faced with multiple opportunities.

Clearing the unimportant things out of the way and finding time when your wishes come up against demands and obligations.

Acting constructively right here and now even when your mind is mired in brooding anxiety.

And in striving for more, also appreciating the value of what you have and what you are.

It is about identifying our inner being and the true values in life.

Finding Focus

The book uses shooting as a metaphor throughout. One reason for this is that shooting, particularly precision shooting and the ability to perform well in this form of sport, requires the same mental capacity as any other form of challenge that is not decided on a physical level. In certain respects, precision shooting differs significantly from most other sports. Just as in countless other sports, it requires incredible discipline and a huge amount of training, good fitness, core stability and excellent balance to reach the world elite. But above all, it requires a well developed mindset, a capacity for self-awareness and for extreme concentration at the right moment, in order just in that moment to rid yourself of disruptive thoughts that interfere with your ability to perform as well as you know you can. Of course this is worth striving for in any sport. So what else makes precision shooting the perfect metaphor when it comes to maintaining focus in life?

Well, for one thing the margins are so terrifyingly small that you can never know ahead of time who is going to go home the victor. This means that shooters are used to losing – it is impossible to win every time. Just like in life, for the most part. We work, struggle and strive, tire and come back fighting in every area of life, always with no real guarantees about the outcome.

Another reason is that precision shooting is a fairly low-key member of the sporting world. We shooters train alone and we have the odd victory here and there, but without any great fanfare. In contrast to most other sports, we win practically nothing apart from an inner joy and pride. And if you think about it, we can see this in all of us as we go through life – constantly working away and dreaming of success on whatever scale. But success will not even get a look in if we can't learn to find the passion in our unseen actions and our hidden efforts. When we do succeed, the praise is often fleeting, and then it is back into obscurity to carry on as normal. And is it not the case that the real, big values of life are rarely given any outward attention? In the sport of rifle shooting, mere millimetres separate first place from 30th, while fractions of a millimetre separate gold and silver. It goes down to decimals in the 10-point circle. A 10 can thus be anything from a 10 on the edge, e.g. 10.0, to a shot dead centre, 10.9. The biathlon, skiing and shooting, offers a good visual comparison. It is "enough" for a biathlete in a standing position to hit any part of the 11.5 centimetre target 50 metres away. For a precision shooter at the same distance the 10-point bullseye is 1.04 cm and hitting anywhere outside this at elite level is considered a miss.

In most sports, to achieve some kind of mental balance, the desire to win has to be balanced with acceptance of losing. In precision shooting, this has to be managed in a situation when the body has to be absolutely still, absolutely relaxed. Adrenaline cannot be allowed to run riot through the muscles. Stress cannot be converted into physical movement. This lasts for over two hours. Sixty shots in a row. During this nervous period, you have to be fully present in the moment, with your complete attention on the current conditions – light, wind, time, tactics, technique and not least your own thoughts.

These instances are just like every other moment of performance where mental rather than physical capacity is the deciding factor.

It is here that the similarities with performance and the capacity to achieve and maintain focus in a context beyond the physical are so striking. Except perhaps when we are running after a stressed colleague in the corridor or chasing after our distracted children, it is rare in our everyday life or in our work that we find ourselves in situations where we also have to move quickly, jump high or run fast.

So what does focus actually mean? And how can we achieve focus? The book's opening pages describe an extreme situation where concentration in the sense of very sharp focus was crucial – my path to the World Championship title. It is extreme in the sense that the experience is not shared very often by other people. Gold in the World Championships is not exactly an everyday occurrence for me either, and so now we are going to focus on focus away from the shooting range.

Focus in the sense of concentration comes most easily when it is built on three conditions: skill, joy and challenge. Skill in something requires plenty of practice and often many years of training. And doing something we are skilled at brings us joy. Add a suitably enticing challenge that we know we can do and all the right conditions are in place.

We now also have the conditions to achieve what is usually referred to as *flow*. This is a state in which we are fully engaged in a task, when notions of time change and an hour can seem like just a few minutes, or vice versa. During this experience of flow, nothing matters but the activity in motion. The subsequent feeling is usually one of happiness, which is why our happiest memories are often of times when we wholeheartedly threw ourselves into a tough challenge that was at the very limit of what we could do. Flow is an experience worth striving for, but it is not absolutely necessary for focus. We can still be focused, which is why it is important not to get hung up on the experience of flow and believe this state is the only way to achieve a focused mind.

When the three conditions come together, our chances of focus are good, whether the task is in a state of flow or not. However, the preconditions for focus tend to come together in people who are doing what they love, and what they have trained for and put a great deal of energy into.

A crystal clear example is the thrill of seeing Michael Jackson on stage. He was performing his passion with an extreme perfection, an indescribable precision in both music and movement. His focus infected everyone watching or dancing, and we were utterly absorbed by his mastery over his body. Whether or not you liked his music, it was hard not to be fascinated by this phenomenal artist and his ability, time after time, to deliver the very best quality with complete focus. And imagine what stamina and copious training lay behind these performances.

With skill, joy and challenge in place, it is thus relatively easy to achieve a high degree of focus, and in the best case, flow. But of course we have to have the opportunity to practise what we love doing without distractions, plus we need the stamina, discipline and strength to train our way up to a certain level of skill. According to psychologist K. Anders Ericsson, a high skill level requires around 10,000 hours of training, which amounts to 20 hours' training a week, 50 weeks a year, for 10 years. To be world champion, this training also has to be of really top quality. The focus thus has to be there from the start, and stay with us all the way *until* we have achieved our desired skill level.

Most of us don't have such training opportunities. They are usually the preserve of the professional sportswoman or performer. Nevertheless, everyday life always brings us unexpected new demands, anxieties, uncertainties and challenges that we haven't predicted or prepared ourselves for. Being able to find focus in these situations is a different challenge from providing peak performance by applying your hard-won skill and your passion. For those who have the capacity to put themselves in a state of focus when performing their major interest, their knowledge of whether or not they are focusing and how they achieve that state plays a pretty minor role. But what happens when they are in a different situation outside their major interest and field of knowledge, outside their comfort zone, and desperately need focus? Can they conjure up this sharp focus in other circumstances where their skills are being put to the test? Or when some unexpected incident or misfortune upsets an otherwise untroubled life? Knowing how to get back into focus, and still be able to perform and draw on inner reserves would certainly be useful in such situations.

Being in a state of focus is not difficult. In fact it is a pleasure. What is difficult is *not* being in that state but *trying* to be. Mastering that is what this book is all about.

However much we want to have control over our focus, we have to start by realising that this phenomenon begins in our brain, and that this is a highly complex part of us over which we don't hold complete power. But understanding what our brain looks like, and what affects our attempts at focus and concentration is a good first step towards better control.

Over the millions of years of our evolution, the brain has gradually increased in size, with our higher brain functions developing out of our lower and older parts. The human brain began developing around 80,000–100,000 years ago, and it was then that we began thinking symbolically and abstractly, looking towards the future.

The most primitive part of our brain is called the reptilian brain. Various emotional centres then grew out of this, and from these came the thinking brain, millions of years later, forming what we would call our intellect. The part of the brain that we think with and that takes care of our intellectual functions thus grew out of the part that controls our emotions. This means that emotions existed long before reason. The older the part of the brain is in the evolutionary process, the more powerful it is, which is why our emotions often win out over our reason.

Our brain reached its current form and function around 40,000–50,000 years ago.

To get a sense of the timescale we can follow Swedish Doctor Nisse Simonson's brilliant example in his book *Hjärnbruk* and convert mankind's time on Earth into a single year. On this scale, we lived as hunter-gatherers right up until 23:45 on 31 December. The industrial revolution came at 23:59:59. The life we live now thus bears very little relationship to the life we were built for. It is therefore perhaps unsurprising that we react to unforeseen, nervous situations at work or at home as if we were threatened by a lion on the savannah.

In such situations, what happens inside the brain is that an incident, or rather a thought about this incident, gains such power that it is interpreted or over-interpreted as a threat to one's life.

A simple way to explain the crucial difference between us intellectual humans and our immediate predecessors is to look at the translation of the Latin scientific names *Homo sapiens* and *Homo sapiens sapiens.* Our species as we are now is called Homo sapiens sapiens, and our immediate predecessor is called Homo sapiens. Homo sapiens means person who knows, while Homo sapiens sapiens means *person who knows that she knows.* This perfectly exemplifies the unique access to consciousness and reflection that only we, modern humans, have been gifted with.

This capacity makes us uniquely placed to plan, structure, question and, via mental images and dreams, shape our lives. This capacity makes it possible, in our minds, to live in the past, the present and the future, in contrast to our ancestors with a less-developed intellect.

It is this ability to think about what just happened, why it happened, or why it failed to work, the capacity to think about how something will happen, or worry that it will not happen, and the ability to wish that we were somewhere else that jolts our mind out of the focus we need in order to function and perform at our best.

Instead of actual threats to our survival, society now surrounds us with demands, efficiencies and productivity. This performance-driven society gives the impression that anything is possible, everything can be made more efficient and we can always become even better. In many ways, this view has a motivating effect on people. But how much better is it possible to become in relation to who we are and what we know, and what does performing at your best actually mean?

We often believe that in a demanding situation we can always perform a little better than we have before. That we can call on our reserves, use our resources to the max and so achieve brilliant solutions, stunning performances or manage to stay focused at work for another few hours. But that is not the case. In mentally demanding situations, we cannot perform any better than the person we already are.

What we should strive for instead is to bring out the innate capacity we already have, and be able to perform as well as we are capable of, as well as we are trained for. No more, no less.

On closer consideration, this happens relatively rarely, probably because we live under the impression that we have to push ourselves to the max when it really counts, and have more faith in ourselves than is reasonable and practicable in the circumstances.

This creates unnecessarily high pressure, which in turn creates poorer conditions for performing at our best. We have a picture of peak performance which hinders rather than helps.

We brood over why something didn't work out as we wanted it to. Nerves, anxiety and fear of embarrassing ourselves or not achieving what we want take over, instead of a composed, focused calm based on the capacity we have spent such a long time building up.

Put simply, distracting thoughts about the past and the future make us unfocused, and this hinders both wellbeing and performance. So can a person learn – when necessary – to rid themselves of these distracting thoughts? And what then? What would it mean in a situation when it really counted? Could this be a way to lift yourself out of a rut and avoid dwelling on failures? Could you, on demand, place yourself in the state in which you perform at your very best?

The answer to the question of how we can liberate our-selves from distracting thoughts, access our innate capabili-ties and focus on the right thing is focus . My own definition of concentration is:

Full focus is being free from distracting thoughts about the future and the past, free from demands and from anxiety.
No doubt. No ifs or buts.
The mind is fully present, and there are no limits to your actual capabilities.

A first step in getting to grips with the phenomenon of focus , and in achieving this state on your own, is to learn what I call the *focus model*. This is a very simple model that I developed during my 25,000 hours at the shooting range. It gives a picture of what happens when we lose focus and how we get it back. The model is a useful tool in our frac-tured modern existence, and it clearly shows the difference between focus and lack of focus .

The background to the model is our capacity to think forwards and backwards in time. How many times have you sat at work but been somewhere else in your head? Thought about what you need to buy for dinner or sneaked a look at your mobile phone? Or as a student with your head in a course book, thought about how much you need to get this reading done rather than actually doing the reading? Or when holding a presentation, nervously thought about all the things you mustn't forget to say, instead of just speaking?

Step one is to take note of *what* you are thinking and *why* in these situations.

Have you considered that distracting and worrying thoughts are often connected to something that has happened, or something that will or might happen? It is these thoughts that disrupt your focus, especially in crucial situations. Before the last shot in finals I, for example, have had thoughts race through my mind such as:

Why did I change ammunition before the start?
Why didn't I do more wind training up in Boden? What if I shoot a 7 with this last shot in the final? What if I fail again?

Step two involves imagining two horizontal timelines with a small gap between them. The left one represents the brain's distracting thoughts about the past. The right one represents the brain's distracting thoughts about the future.

The gap between the lines provides space for a "now".

PAST   **FUTURE**

Step three, once you have decided whether your distracting thoughts belong to the past or the future, is to imagine placing them on either the past line or the future line.

Step four is now to cross out or simply get rid of all the distracting thoughts for a moment. But how? The trick is to use your own mental powers to replace these thoughts about the past or the future with a thought that places the mind in the immediate present, in the "now". It should be one little neutral thought that doesn't make you dwell on anything at all, either forwards or backwards in time. Like "a leaf". Of course this is easier said than done, but herein lies the secret to the art of focus.

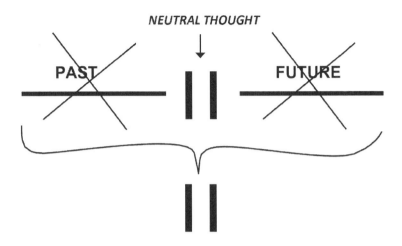

The figure above describes the situation when distracting thoughts about both the past and the future are removed for a moment. Anxiety about the future, how things are going to go, is gone. Likewise, no dwelling on what has already happened. The mind is uncluttered and sharp, and our true ability is uninhibited by either thoughts that create stress, shame or anxiety or thoughts that take us away from the present. It is in this state that we are as good as we can be. As good as we are trained for. We can't be any better in this moment. We find ourselves in "the now", with absolute presence and absolute focus.

Particularly in situations when it really counts, the anxiety we create for ourselves has the same effect on us as the real threats to survival that were part of our ancestors' lives. We act with the "fight or flight response". The mind's anxious thoughts about what if…, about the *future* in the focus model, affect our emotional system, which takes charge of the brain and lets the body react as if we were being chased by a lion and threatened with death. The body makes itself ready to fight or flee, so the focus is on powerful physical movement instead of the fine motor or intellectual performance we were about to accomplish. In physically demanding sports, the hit of adrenalin and fast heartbeat is often a bonus for performance. But even though a certain amount of nerves always heighten one's focus, too much adrenalin has the opposite effect in mentally demanding situations – for example in circumstances that require fine motor skills, such as shooting, and contexts such as giving a presentation or a speech, focusing on the person speaking to you, being interviewed and being sure about saying the right thing, when composed, fine movements are good for performance:

Damn, I've forgotten what I was supposed to say....! What's my manager going to say if I can't explain...? Why didn't I say what I thought I should say? If I don't get my message across now, the whole deal will collapse...

Think for a moment, read the sentences above again, and note that they all have a connection with the past or the future. Dwelling either on something that was thought before or on an image of what will happen if...

If the mind can be freed from thoughts like those above, the chances of achieving a state of focus are high, and this increases the opportunity to unleash more of your inner energy, creativity and focus on the performance.

The "now" that the focus model shows is a period of a few seconds, often just milliseconds, which is enough on any given occasion to achieve the focus level needed in order to function and perform at your best and be fully present in the moment. The mind learns to "move in and out" of this state, which is why such focus can also be maintained over a longer period.

Between the states of high focus and presence, thoughts about the past and the future, both worrying and reflective, are naturally of great value to us. But not in that moment. Not when we need to perform at our very best. Not when a pattern of distracting thoughts has to be broken. In that moment, the mind has to be able to shift into focus.

When we are consciously shifting into focus (controlled focus) – which is far more difficult than shifting out of focus (automatic focus) – we should be aware that the brain has the capacity to shift focus incredibly quickly. However, it is basically only able to think about and focus on one thing at a time. This should be seen as an asset, whereby one thought, like the autumn leaf in my opening story, which crowds out other thoughts for a moment, is enough to achieve focus. In this context it is easy to believe that it is important to think the *right* thought – a thought that is related to the task in hand, something you should not forget, something that helps with performance. In shooting, the thought might be expected to be: "keep still", and in a speech: "I also want to thank…". But it has been proven that *what* you think is not actually important. In principle, the neutral thought could be absolutely anything. The most important point is that it breaks the pattern and removes the distracting thoughts. Our brain doesn't forget what we know, what we are supposed to be doing and everything we want to say, just because a neutral thought pops up. On the contrary, if all thoughts are removed for a while, we open up our consciousness to deliver its creative and often very smart view of the situation.

The point here is a powerful one: If you can achieve this state of focus , and a millisecond is enough, removing distracting thoughts and replacing them with a non-distracting thought that keeps the mind present, you have the capability on every occasion when you are heading into a pattern of poor focus, stress, dwelling or concern to actually break this trend. This enables you, in the short and long term, to steer the situation and your life in the right direction – whether it is for a specific task or for a long-range task or goal. You are quite simply able to focus, and that is worth its weight in gold, not only for World Championship finals but also over the longer perspective.

What the focus model represents is thus a simple, visual explanation of an otherwise very complex system in our brain. In the book's various chapters, you will notice that the focus model is the starting point for all the arguments, and one of the cornerstones that builds a life in focus.

The model helps you, in a clear way, to notice whether or not your thoughts are unfocused. The first step towards this is to identify whether they have a link with the past or the future. Learning to recognise your own thoughts, where they come from and why is one of the conditions for achieving this state.

Now we know something about what our intelligent brain does in situations when it really counts, and we also know that in principle the brain only has the capacity to think one thought at a time. It can easily switch quickly from one thought to another but it "sees", or rather notices, only one thing at a time.

We should also draw a distinction between *automatic focus* and *controlled focus*. The automatic focus reacts to something that suddenly happens nearby – for example when an animal jumps out into the road, or a ping from your mobile phone, this instantly draws your focus. The controlled version, on the other hand, has a focus until we notice something, and even then it stays on what we are focusing on. An example is my continued attention on the target, my breathing and my finger on the trigger, despite a stern judge in a yellow vest passing me on the shooting range. Easily explained automatic focus is unconscious. Controlled focus is conscious.

From a broader and longer perspective, the value of controlled focus extends far beyond the moment. In contrast to the automatic focus, which is happy to skip from one thing to another, the controlled form can keep us focused on what we have chosen to focus on, despite surrounding changes, setbacks, new competition or tempting distractions. In other words, it is closely related to both patience and persistence.

With this in mind, let us do a very simple practical experiment.

Imagine you're sitting on a red blanket on a sandy beach on a really warm and lovely summer's day. In a little basket you have coffee in a flask and some delicious biscuits and grapes. You're looking out to sea, watching a yacht sail on the horizon.

Now keep your focus on this image of yourself on the red blanket on the beach, the coffee, the biscuits, the grapes and the yacht in the distance. Ignore the guy down at the water's edge pulling an ice cream cart with a Magnum sign. Don't think about the Magnum now.

You see yourself on the red blanket on the beach, the basket, coffee, biscuits and grapes and the yacht in the distance – with no Magnum in your hand.

So: did you at any point think of a Magnum ice cream?

Anyone who didn't think of ice cream must have a special gift, or rather a mental deficiency, as it is a perfectly normal reaction for a functioning brain as soon as the eye

reads "ice cream" or "Magnum". I usually do this experiment in front of a group of people with their eyes closed.
The fun thing about this is that most of them are hanging
on my every word and really want to focus , so when I ask
them not to think about the ice cream cart and Magnums,
they are so amazed that almost all of them open their
eyes and look at me as if I have just landed from a far-off
planet.

This is a simple way to illustrate how the brain works,
and how quickly it switches from one image to another. It is
good to know this, since it also explains how any thought at
all can affect the brain – even thoughts we barely have time
to register have an effect, sometimes positive, sometimes
negative. This is why we often find ourselves automatically
doing what we think we shouldn't do. If you think "don't
shoot a seven to the left", this actually significantly increases
the risk of actually doing so. The thought or image of an
autumn leaf, on the other hand, improves the chances of
pulling off a good shot, because the brain is not being disturbed by any distracting thoughts that shift the focus.

It is possible to train up your controlled or focus. It is
therefore possible to train your brain to retain an image
for as long as possible and, after being distracted, return
as quickly as possible to the original image, such as the
ice cream-free beach experience. Now you are able to consciously achieve focus, controlled focus. I leave the theory of
how this works to those who know immeasurably more about
neurology than I do. But to refer back to Ericsson's 10,000
hours, it is clear that few of us are able to channel so much
time into what we want to become good at. However, there
is one thing that each of is guaranteed to have done and
will do at least 20 hours a week – and that is think. So here
at least we have a chance to excel! Instead of commanding

ourselves to "not think about ice cream", we can give fuel to one of the existing images and repeat, for example, "yacht". This pushes out the image of ice cream, even if just for a second. But the effect is still surprisingly clear.

One tip on how you can practise and learn to switch focus in this way when the pressure is on is "Roger's notes".

Roger was one of my closest training buddies. He had been shooting since he was really young and he was technically incredibly gifted. He set a perfect example on the range – methodical, balanced and relaxed, with a purity of style.

Despite his experience and a number of Olympic Games under his belt, Roger had still not made an international breakthrough and won international championship medals. He was therefore driven to perform even better and found he was being held back not by his technique but by his mind.

To try and get Roger into the necessary state of focus in pressured situations, I invented the method that I call *Roger's notes.*

The exercise involved me one day writing entirely unrelated words on small notes – for example "door handle", "banana", "watering can", "fish finger", "toaster". These were then placed upside down next to the spot where Roger would be shooting.

Roger began his match and was now instructed to carefully take note of *when* his distracting thoughts began taking the form of doubt and anxiety, *when* thoughts unrelated to the task in hand began appearing: *What if I shoot a seven to the right and miss out on the final...* In this state of poor focus Roger took a short pause and simply turned over the top note in the pile and read the word "toaster".

The next shot – bang – a 10.

Just as in the focus model, one neutral thought erased all of Roger's anxious thoughts about the past and the future. In this state, for a few seconds he was able to focus on the task with just "toaster" in his mind – an irrelevant word, a mental image with no emotional loading, but one that helped the brain to free itself from all the pressing thoughts that were on his mind. Free from the distracting thoughts that make a task you are fully trained for turn into a scenario of complete anxiety.

"Toaster" helped Roger to break the pattern and achieve a state in which, even if just for a moment, he was able to focus and perform as well as he was actually trained for. Focus in all its simplicity.

If all it took to achieve a life of focus was to think about autumn leaves or a toaster, I would end the book right here. The idea behind the autumn leaves and toaster is simple and very effective, but it is not enough on its own to obtain a life in focus. Over the longer term, needing to think toaster as soon as we lose focus could become rather wearing. It should be seen as a trick to apply when the pressure is high in a demanding situation, at work, at home or maybe on the golf course. An example to keep in mind as a reminder of the focus model and how we work. The goal in fact is not to need Roger's notes very often, which is why we will continue the book by looking more closely at the parts of our life and our existence that influence our capacity to achieve focus.

But before we delve into this, we will reflect on the value of concentration, going beyond the examples we have already seen. What is the point of greater focus when we are not in a World Championship final or on stage in front of

75,000 people at Wembley Stadium? What role does focus play in an ordinary day at the office for example?

First and foremost, just how present are we at meetings? Do we look forward to them, or do we attend them out of duty, while thinking about anything but the subject of the meeting? Imagine what would happen if everyone was allowed to finish up whatever they were doing on their computer or phone before the meeting got started. It is highly likely that presence and interest in the meeting's agenda would improve substantially. Unfortunately, the problem with this policy is that most of us have too much to do, so very few of us would ever be ready for the meeting.

What if all meetings in a company or organisation had higher focus levels, with a *presence* of at least 80 percent? What I mean by this is that at least 80 percent of the meeting participants' thoughts are focused on the meeting and its content rather than all sorts of other things, instead of the current estimated average of barely 40 percent. What effect would this generate within the organisation?

And then there is the eternal email problem... How many of us, just before lunch, worriedly look at our watch and realise that the number of unanswered emails in our inbox has not even been halved yet, and so we spend the rest of the day with them preying on our minds? Maybe we need to get to work at five in the morning and clear our inbox before the working day even starts? That is all very well, but then who is going to take the kids to preschool, make breakfast or walk the dog, and how many more emails would such a dutiful action generate? Coping or not coping with emails is one thing, but true focus is about being able to free ourselves from dwelling on those e-mails we haven't got round to.

Another enemy of focus is all the times at work we spend being irritated by others. How often is our attention distracted by frustration with a colleague who never delivers on time, thinks he knows everything or talks about people behind their back? Can such frustrations be avoided? No, probably not, and this is also probably not something to strive for. Differences, different ways of thinking and the fact that most of us put ourselves first are part and parcel of human behaviour. If, however, we begin to think about how many of our thoughts dwell on this, and imagine that these thoughts could be cleared away for a moment, what would happen then?

What would happen if slightly less of our brainpower was spent pleasing those around us or our line manager, and a little more was channelled into what we actually believe in? If more of us felt involved in a larger context and were happy to focus more on the best interests of the company or the organisation, instead of our own personal gain, advancement or position, what would happen then?

What would it mean if we became a touch better at focusing on the work in hand right now, and not letting it be affected by thoughts about where the last project or the last meeting went awry?

Or if we could keep our mind on real, but perhaps heavy-going, tasks and spend less time in a rose-tinted dream world where everything goes without a hitch?

A general question concerning focus at work is thus how much quality and focus is wasted due to thoughts in no way related to the task in hand.

A school head to whom I spoke a while ago reflected that 2014 was the year he worked by far the most hours, but when he looked at what he had actually achieved in that time, "it was almost frightening".

This quotation sums up the situation for many of us, not just professionally but also privately. We are committed, we work hard and get a lot done but, if we think about it, we could have done it all with a little greater focus and a little greater presence. The thin line between focus and lack of focus means that we so rarely function as well as we could.

One can also talk about focus over a *long-term perspective*. Many are good at focusing in the short term, often under time pressure. I am thinking here about all the students who choose to leave their exam revision until the last moment, for example, and the many key decisions that are taken in acute emergency situations. "Quick decisions with a quick response" are what our brains are happiest with. The common feature of this type of focus is that it is followed by rapid feedback, an almost immediate reward for one's efforts.

But where can we find our long-term focus? The one that steers a life, a whole organisation or a whole world in the right direction? It is a tough ask to focus for a long period of time on something that requires a long-term focus and that is more important than all our everyday firefighting, on something that only brings rewards much later, maybe generations later.

Despite our unique capacity to think long-term, we want a response to what we do *now*. Look at the way we start cleaning our home instead of tackling that big project with the deadline in a few weeks' time. Look at how easily we turn to work instead of getting to grips with a private issue that is bubbling away under the surface.

Look at the politicians who are more focused on being re-elected than on what needs to be done to secure the future for the next generation.

Look at how terrible I thought the losses were in the first few years, before I learned to take the long view. A sporting career can seem long and impressive. But by and large it is actually quite short, just a small part of a bigger picture.

The desire to be rewarded for one's efforts is very human and not something to be overlooked. But what happens if we learn to apply a somewhat longer perspective? If we learn to delay our reward, and learn to steer our focus towards things that benefit others as well as ourselves? If politics more frequently looked beyond national interests, and if more people could enjoy being involved in a global context rather than an individual and only temporarily gratifying one?

This book identifies four themes that are most important to the art of focus: state of mind, objectives, self-worth and failure.

To attach some sort of structure and order to my argument, I will be outlining five types of focus, by which I mean four types of *challenges* that in different contexts affect and require our attention.

These five types encompass focus from a short and long perspective:

- Sharp focus under pressure (championship final, giving a speech)
- Relaxed focus (thoughtlessness)
- Focus in the sense of presence (in a meeting at work, at the kitchen table at home)
- Focus during drudgery/boredom (three hours of shooting practice, exam revision, writing long reports)

- Focus for life (steering your efforts, your week, your life in the right direction)

The focus that falls within the framework of the short perspective is sharp focus under pressure, focus in the sense of presence and relaxed focus. Focus during drudgery/boredom may fall into both the shorter and longer perspective focus for life belongs absolutely to the longer perspective.

WHAT TO FOCUS ON?

What is it around us that affects our focus? And how can
we achieve focus when we most need it?

We have learned that focus has five characteristics.– two
of these appear to have the greatest impact on and meaning for us, a sharp focus and a relaxed one. One of them we
have looked at: full focus during a specific and demanding
task over a very short period. The other is the focus that
is about just being and in principle not thinking at all, a
deeper state that lasts a long time. Call this mindfulness,
daydreaming, deep focus or whatever else you want. I call it
relaxed focus.

Being focused on one task, for example when dancing, deep in an exciting book, out digging in a flowerbed
or pushing yourself in a training session, is about being in
a state where there is no space for distracting thoughts or
an attempt to perform anything except what you are actually doing. Being immersed in a task frees you from anxiety
and brooding and puts you effortlessly in the here and now.
There is no space for other thoughts. This is where we want
to be in those moments when we need to think clearly or
stop dwelling on how something went or how it might go.
This state, relaxed focus, appears difficult to achieve on
command without effort. But the more effort we put in, the
further we get from this focus. The fact is that as soon as we

begin straining to focus, the battle is lost. We have to simply let this state establish itself, without any direct attempt to be either focused or adept.

For most of us, those moments in the day when we don't need to achieve anything, and we allow ourselves a moment of unconfined reflection, are treasured but few and far between. Most of us would like to have more of these times, particularly as we know there is evidence that these moments of daydreaming, when our subconscious is active but our conscious intellect is still, are terribly important for our wellbeing and for our intuition, our creativity and our good ideas. It doesn't matter whether these occasions are created when we lean back in an office chair and switch off from the computer and all the meetings for a while, head off to our summer cottage for a day, potter in the garden or hear nothing but the crunching sound underfoot as we walk to the metro station. The main thing is that we allow ourselves these moments of "thoughtlessness". This is where our smart thoughts are born, and the most complex musings fall into place. Although we don't notice any effort, our subconscious takes care of much that we would otherwise have been forced to try and clear up. We are now in the middle point of the focus model, just like in a pressured situation when we think of a toaster so as not to get stuck on thoughts of past and present, on demands and anxieties.

There is a distinct risk that when we have that desired moment of peace, in our office chair or on the way to the metro, there is so much we haven't had time to resolve or think through during the day, that we are unable to immerse ourselves in a genuine state of thoughtlessness. Instead, this unique moment becomes yet another time to *think*, in order to achieve something that we believe requires our conscious thought. We don't dare to let go of the control we have, or think we have, over our thoughts. We believe our conscious thoughts are the same thing as our intelligence. But the brain's subconscious has access to infinitely more thoughts, memories and creative solutions than our conscious mind. In actual fact, it is often all these *attempts* to think with concrete clarity that block us from the boundless intelligence that resides in our subconscious. It is a daunting prospect to let go of all the thoughts buzzing around and all the attempts to perform during a vital task and instead picture a toaster in front of you, and to lean back in the middle of the day and clear your mind when there is so much to do and so much to think about.

These two types of focus that we have now examined, one sharp and one relaxed might come across as contradictory. Sharp, lightning fast and conscious focus in a specific and important situation to some extent disrupts the brain's capacity, on another occasion and for a little longer time, to be unconscious, relaxed and "thoughtless". Research has shown that the sharp , conscious focus takes up a smaller, more localised part of the brain than the relaxed, creative, daydreaming and subconscious focus, which activates a larger and broader section of the brain. Thinking only conscious thoughts blocks access to our deeper subconscious, which is at least as able to generate incisive thoughts as our conscious mind. Sharp and conscious focus and relaxed unconscious focus both have an effect on our capacity to perform and function as well as we can. They both provide free passage to the powers of our complex brain. Both free us from anxiety. So can one become skilled at both forms of focus, the sharp intensive one and the rather longer relaxed form? The fact is that by getting good at the one, you automatically become good at the other. They are actually the same thing, they just happen at different times and under different degrees of consciousness. Consider this illustration:

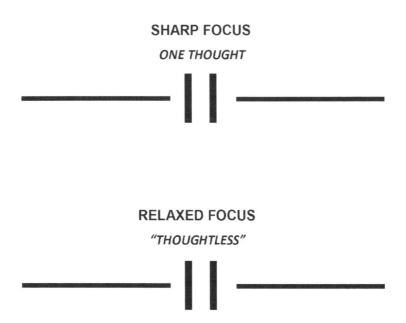

SHARP FOCUS

ONE THOUGHT

RELAXED FOCUS

"THOUGHTLESS"

Understanding whether you are or are not focusing, be it focusing on a difficult task or being "thoughtless" in your office chair, is about noticing whether or not you are exerting yourself. Focus, both the sharp, intensive and the, relaxed form, takes no effort. The difficult thing, as mentioned before, is achieving a state of focus without *trying* to.

It would seem that in sociocultural terms we have a picture of what focus is and what it looks like. We see a sportswoman's fixed look before her performance, or the hard look of the politicians who emerge from days of negotiations to speak to the media, as crystal clear pictures of focus. But consider for a moment the times we have seen the most magnificent feats and performances, or when you yourself have done something you recall being particularly outstanding. In this moment, you probably had quite a relaxed look on your face. You probably trained hard for the occasion in question, but in the moment you set aside all attempts to be better than you actually are. You just were.

Imagine, in the middle of an important task, that something disrupts your focus. You notice the effort involved in trying to regain your focus in these distracting surroundings, or rather: *your* distracting thoughts *about* the surroundings pop into your head all the time. Frustration grows and the exertion becomes increasingly noticeable. The greater the exertion and the harder you try, the further you drift away from a state of focus. So what can you do?

In my case, I think about the man in the red jacket. The first time I saw him was on a bench many years ago. He was amazingly good-looking and exuded a charm that must have been attractive to everyone in his orbit. We acknowledged each other with a polite little nod a few times a year at various matches, in various locations around the world. Significantly older than me and manager of the Austrian team, he was not someone I would spontaneously approach and I therefore maintained a sophisticated distance.

Winning gold at the World Championships helped. At a social gathering in a beautifully decorated hangar in Thun, Switzerland, which accompanied the medal ceremony, I randomly ended up in the same group of people as him. This was due to their interest in my final shot in the match – 10.9. He listened intently as I talked and glowed like the sun. I then felt obliged to mingle and so moved on to join the next group. As I was leaving the hangar later on, high on the atmosphere and the unusual but wonderful feeling of being here as a winner, a car crept up behind me. The driver's window slid down and I heard: "May I have the honour of escorting the new world champion to her quarters?"

I knew straight away that it was him, the Austrian, and I didn't hesitate for a second. In that moment, I was just as focused and dedicated as earlier in the day when I had taken my nervous shot for gold. The difference was that I wore a permanent smile like a split tomato.

The next time I saw him was a few months later. One chilly morning in Austria I was on the shooting range, well prepared, structured and focused. I had new shooting glasses for this competition, the most expensive on the market and recently trialled in Germany. They sat, carefully polished, on the little stool in front of me and I was ready to begin shooting in a standing position. This was after an encouraging score of 198 points in a prone position. Well aware that I was top of the leader board, I was proud, motivated and appropriately nervous. Just as I should be. I had practised the standing position extensively and ought to be ready to hit a number of 10s in the first round without any major missteps, bearing in mind the good start to the match.

There was a good grouping to the sighting shots, and I took the always tricky decision to commence the match series, raised my rifle and stood for a while in a steady position, waiting for the wind. I lowered the barrel that last millimetre, took aim, squeezed the trigger and fired a shot that I followed in my mind's eye far beyond the target. Textbook reactions – nervous but cool. I kept my nerves under control and continued in that vein, hitting 10 after 10. My aim was steady. I looked at the shooting bench, at the ammunition box, loaded mechanically the same way every time and lifted the barrel with precision. I presented such a convincing picture of success that people started gathering behind me to see the next 10 flash up on the screen.

After six 10s in a row, I had built up a significant lead. I adjusted my glasses, mostly for the sake of appearances, and in my peripheral vision I saw a man in a red jacket join the group behind me. He somehow broke the pattern. He was there just like all the others, but his jacket was irritatingly red. It shone as brightly as the interest in my next shot from the person wearing it. It was him! The man I so longed to talk to again. The man I had spent more time thinking about than I probably should have. Now he was behind me, watching my match. A warmth rose up inside me, perhaps even a smile and a pride that he had come to see me. But why now? Why not in the canteen, on the running track or in some shuttle bus on the way to training? We had already been here for several days and he waits until now to enter my carefully prepared life – dressed in a glaringly red jacket? I was disturbed by the fact that he had appeared unexpectedly during the match, an irritation that mixed with the warm feeling inside. However much I kept my eye on my chosen focus and outwardly maintained my composure, the bright red kept cutting through. My heart thumped, crying out for more space in my body. I pretended as if nothing had distracted me and tried to look as if I was concentrating. Tensely, I raised the barrel again and fell into the well rehearsed routine: stood stock still, analysed the wind and the barrel's position, maintained this elegant position with the sight ring perfectly placed around the 10 second after second. But he was behind me, amongst all the other expectant faces. He was in my head. Awareness of his presence got the upper hand. Conviction about another 10 no longer dominated my mind. The attempt to keep myself calm and focused was valiant but completely pointless. Who was I playing this role for? Why not just show the world the truth? Here I stood, trying to hit a 12 millimetre target from

50 metres away in variable wind with the pressure on to per-form well, but completely out of focus because of him, the stylish guy in the red jacket next to the Englishman with the curly beard. Why not surrender to the overwhelming force within and behind me, lay down my rifle, take off my shooting glasses, turn around and shoot a dazzling smile right into his lovely eyes? There was nothing I wanted more.

My thoughts were all over the place and the fraud I was perpetrating made me want to laugh – all these people were standing here, watching keenly and believing that I was focused and completely unmoved. So I squeezed the trigger and fired just as I had done a thousand times before, but this time with him in my head and a cramp-like tension in my body. So I finally fired my seventh shot in the series and continued to act as if everything was under control – but the screen failed to flash up a 10. A 7 right out to the left. Jesus, a 7! A murmur rippled through the crowd behind me and my stomach tightened with shame and distress. I couldn't miss many more if I was going to hold onto the lead. But of course this miss was followed by another one. Now my heart was beating less fast. Instead, a lump had taken root in my throat. I lowered my head and let two large tears roll from my eyes. It was sad. It was embarrassing. I no longer fought to win, and barely even to retain my honour, but to keep the rest of the tears back until the match was over. The audience behind me dispersed and all that was left was one red and one blue and yellow jacket, the stylish Austrian and my coach. He thought he had spotted a technical detail to explain the devastating 7 that proved the turning point in a match that could have ended in success. (This is how things go in most matches, if not practically all of them – they could have ended in success but very few actually do.) The challenge for a coach is that they can't read minds, which makes their task of identifying the causes of both success and failure a real challenge. A fantastically honed technique can rescue a lot, but clearly not everything. At least not in my case. My focus was blown apart when Mr Red Jacket slipped into the crowd behind me. Notably the real concern here was not the presence of Mr Red Jacket, but my own thoughts about him and the worry over how I could now work this issue through; it was not the colour red, but my mental capacity to identify the reason why I could no longer perform to my best ability. The blame may have related to Mr Red Jacket but I gradually came to a forgiving understanding of why things turned out the way they did. In actual fact the issue was simply that my curiosity and my feelings for the man in the red jacket were far stronger than my ability to focus exclusively on the shooting bench, the barrel, the sight, the wind and the target.

The man in the red jacket later became a really close friend and we shared many moments of wisdom. Ever since, catching a glimpse of Mr Red Jacket behind me on the shooting range has been a bonus, a warm feeling that no longer disturbs my focus and prevents me from doing my best. The lesson I learned is that the harder I try to focus, the less focused I get, and that certain forces around us are stronger than those we can create for ourselves with our various methods and techniques, no matter how hard we try. What I should have done was surrender to this passion and in the name of honesty I should have done what I couldn't stop thinking about. I should have realised and accepted that my emotions had overwhelmed my common sense and gone with it. I should have stopped struggling to regain my focus, and I should definitely not have pretended to be unmoved It was all an act, but to no avail. A one-minute time-out would have been enough to let the chaos from my brain's emotional centre run free and then regain control over my thoughts.

The point of the story is to note that the situation would (once again) have been improved by *noticing* when one's emotions are such that they should be given free rein. The aim is to stop trying to achieve focus and instead let go for a moment, before returning to the task in hand, free from exertion. Strong feelings of joy, grief and love are examples of emotions that should be given some space when they unexpectedly pop up in situations that we feel are important. Accept them as so fundamental for our species that it would be arrogant to believe they could be wiped from your mind for even a moment. Try to reach the middle of the focus model, and act in a way that frees you from thoughts about *what if...?*, no matter what it takes to get there. To interrupt the match, at least on a mental level, and give the Austrian a smile would have been to welcome focus with open arms, even though it would have been a focus on the "wrong thing". In that moment, I should have given up on the huge effort of trying to remain focused on the "right" thing and instead been present in an alternate reality, before composing myself and returning to the "right" thing, the actual task in hand.

It is when we just exist and accept things as they are that we are most concentrated and do what we do with the utmost focus. How well we complete a specific task or project depends on how well prepared and trained we are, not how hard we push our mind at the time.

We tend to push ourselves to be good and to perform at our best. And thank goodness we are equipped with this drive and with the capacity to feel joy when we succeed. The question is, where should most of that effort be invested? In the actual performance or beforehand? Perseverance, stamina and patience are characteristics that, if you think about it, all have their effect *before* a performance or a final objective: a good term of study, a successful sports season or preparations for a presentation. These characteristics not only steer us in the right direction and towards a strong work ethic, but also help to keep up the quality of what is being done. If we constantly apply these, we lay a solid foundation for good results and are better *prepared* for a challenge than we think. Focus and exertion should thus be invested in ongoing, well executed work before a challenge. If we have honestly prepared ourselves, we also find it easier to achieve a state of focus when it counts, without any exertion. In this context, the key is to trust in your acquired knowledge and capabilities, and not in some sort of ineffective fighting spirit. It is said that the brain is like a muscle and that it can be trained in the same way. This is a fine metaphor, but not one to blindly rely on. When it comes to the brain, this image should only apply to training *before* the actual moment of mental performance. Given enough time, the primary memory can be trained just like a muscle. The trickier task is to force the memory to be better in a specific demanding situation. A muscle is at its most powerful when being pushed to maximum exertion – think bench presses – but that is not the case with the mind. We can't fight our way to focus in mental challenges that require no physical exertion. That just makes us more and more what we don't want to be – distracted. Trying to struggle free from thoughts about Mr Red Jacket was the worst strategy I could have chosen.

Being well prepared and able to resist exerting ourselves when it counts provides good conditions for achieving focus.

This requires a capacity to trust your own capabilities, and an awareness that getting to this point has taken concentration, patience and perseverance – not masses of hard work with no focus.

Remarkably, we often still work extra hard, far too hard, to really make sure that nothing is left to chance. I heard this at many different training camps, for example. It was like a mantra that all elite sportsmen and women lived by – nothing can be left to chance, nothing can go wrong, and so it is always best to put in another couple of hours' training. Quality was often overlooked in the amount of training we all strove for, and to a large extent were judged by. To be among the world's best, 35,000–40,000 shots a year is hardly enough and 2,000 hours of training is a bare minimum. If you can't present these figures to the national team managers and the Olympic Committee, you are going to struggle. But having performed such wonders for a couple of years, it turned out that daring to leave the odd thing to chance was the wisest move of all. At least when there were medals to play for.

Roger and I regularly organised our own little training camps together. As usual over the winter, we made our way to the indoor arena in Helsingborg one weekend. We spent these weekends in a basement, where we stuck to a strict regime. We allowed ourselves to emerge from the hall twice a day to buy a sandwich in the cafeteria on the ground floor and see some daylight. We trained like crazy and no doubt improved. In the world of shooting there is a well known expression for those times when the 10s are proving elusive: "I don't have enough shots in my body." And of course the only cure for such a condition is practice, practice, practice, which is why we shot as much as we could. Come Sunday evening, as we tidied up the hall and cleared up buckets full of empty shells, we were proud as punch at the number of shots we had managed to fire over these few days.

And then one day I broke the pattern. The plan was for Roger to practise the standing position and for me to practise kneeling. Behind the shooting lanes there was a small room with a table and chairs, shooting paraphernalia in a box and results tables on the walls. A window looking out onto the range allowed me to watch Roger, who had already got started in his lane. I stayed in the room, with my rifle on the table ready for me to complete my usual routine of assembling it according to my technical notes. There is a specific setting for prone, one for standing and one from kneeling. I stood looking at the rifle, wondering what would happen to the centre of gravity if I moved the sling swivel a millimetre forwards or backwards. Then I went through the same thinking with the lower part of the recoil pad and the position of the diopter. I continued with these thoughts for as long as they lasted. I did some little stretching exercises and then sat for a while looking at the results tables on the walls and musing about all the youngsters who had battled away in this little hall every Wednesday.

My eyes drifted to Roger, who was still standing there, shooting. It seems to be going well, I thought. Then I put all my energy into my kneeling position and tried an exercise I had never done before: I focused intently on just five shots. Two hours had passed and before I was even ready to get into my lane I met Roger's flat gaze in the doorway. Things had not gone very well out there. Sweaty, flushed and with a mark on his cheek from the butt, he explained with a sigh that it pulled to the right every time, but he had at least managed 120 shots. After water, fruit and a brief rest, he was back in position on the range. I continued pottering about with my rifle, but in a great mood and with a growing, pleasing sense of focus. I then went and set myself up in the kneeling position on the range without firing a single shot. I worked on my motor skills and on tiny adjustments to the centre of gravity. While Roger shot off another box of 60 cartridges, I took a break and looked at the youngsters' results tables again. Towards lunchtime I finally took my five shots, which were of the highest quality. I executed them with such extreme focus that to this day I can recall every shot. I was as happy and ridiculously pleased as it is possible to be when something turns out better than you had ever dreamed. After these 10s, I was able to write in my notebook that I had learned about the correlation between quality and focus, about opening up to chance and letting it divert me from my predetermined plan. About being proud of the quality, not the quantity. Without any great mental effort, that morning I exhibited a combination of relaxed focus and sharp focus: long periods of thoughtlessness and deep reflection in the little room, followed by quick, razor-sharp focus for a short period out on the range.

With fewer shots in my body than planned and with this latest lesson in mind, I went on to win a prestigious competition in Australia. Quantity is good as long as it includes quality. In other words, as long as it includes focus. But however much we want to be well trained and focused, there is a limit. The brain is unable to maintain focus for several hours at a time. We all know that. But there is something fishy about this notion of quantity. We often train extra hard, work extra hard, fill our time with matters of importance and show huge commitment, without becoming very much better, or without getting the results we expect considering the time we have put in. Isn't this a little odd? As ever, this is often rooted in the classic anxiety about not performing well enough. A kind of comfort and pride comes from the commitment and the hard work we have done. After all, that is something we can control. It is more difficult to exercise control over the end goal or the upcoming performance, and that is an unpalatable fact. We put our energies into what we can control and definitely influence. It is the hard work, the late nights and the busy calendar that we and others see and can ascribe to our character en route to our objective. It is common to seek solace in the notion that "even if it all goes wrong, at least I worked hard". Failing *and* not having trained properly would cause a complete loss of face.

But it is worth bearing in mind here that no one but us can know whether the work or the training we do is fully focused. Only you know for sure whether you are focused on what you are doing. Genuine focus is difficult to see on the outside. It is difficult to formulate requirements for. The truth is that it is easier for a national team manager and an employer to set requirements regarding training and working hours. We think we know what focus looks like, but it is actually a rather hidden phenomenon. Nevertheless, we all have a talent for *acting* focused. The exertion, which we sometimes misinterpret as high focus, instead comes from *trying* not to betray our anxieties. In this state, naturally enough, most of our thoughts are about trying to maintain the illusion that we are not in the least bit worried. And this puts our thoughts anywhere but in the middle of the focus model. They are dwelling on what mustn't happen, instead of being in the moment, which allows our anxieties to take over.

It is also worth reflecting on quantity versus quality when planning our lives and filling our diaries. We even give a name to the empty spaces that we take great pains to create in the diary, such as quality time, which puts pressure on the mind that in these moments too we should be doing something sensible.

My own favourite expression in this context was coined when I was replying to a journalist, who had asked how I have the time to train, compete and work. After a brief moment of consideration, I answered warmly but firmly: "I have the time because there is so much I *don't* need to do."

This means that the time freed up should not be filled with more training or more work, but should remain just free time. Being aware of your own thoughts and why you are thinking them is, as we have learned, fundamental in developing our capacity to focus. And this takes time.

Let me return to the day I decided to become the best at one thing. It is pertinent at this point to ask whether all the time and effort I put into this one thing had any value, beyond the odd medal here and there and the fact that I eventually achieved my goal? One might think that, having become so good at one thing and sidelined so much more, I would be very bad at a lot of other things. Counter-intuitively, that seems not to be the case. Being very good at one thing will almost always make you good at other things too. Now I would like to make it very clear that I am not a world champion in any sport other than shooting, and I am unlikely to end up being a master chef or a leading mathematician either, but as regards the things I generally pushed to the side as less of a priority, I am not as useless as might be expected. Those who do one thing well, and who manage to clear everything else out of the way, possess a kind of tested perseverance that the mind has been trained to work with. The brain learns to find focus in the most mundane contexts – and this is an advantage that is well worth having. This capacity bleeds into every other context in life that requires a little more than just your everyday brainpower. It is an asset when your manager assigns you a long task of the most boring kind, when your own goal requires long-term training or when life takes an unexpectedly sad turn. Practising this capacity is perhaps more difficult nowadays, as we can always make new choices and so stimulate and constantly challenge the mind. But that is not to say it can't be done. It is at least a smarter approach than trying to change your intense external circumstances or the times we live in. Things are how they are, and that is fine. We need to deal with the situation as it is, and to the best of our ability be both happy and focused within it. Understanding focus and reclaiming this ability is a more sustainable approach to today´s challenges than digital detox for example.

The endless possibilities that swirl around us have created the attitude that life must be lived intensively. There is so much that has to be done in the time we have available, which in turn has created the idea that life is short. This makes deprioritising and focusing on just one thing even more unsettling and almost a little frightening. Instead we do as much as we can and try to pack in everything we want to do while we are able. What's more, we first do what we believe we have to do so that we can then turn to what we really want to do. And this makes time pass quickly. Or at least it feels that way.

The fact that many of us are good at multitasking does not mean that what we do at the same time as something else is good. It is actually quite rare nowadays that we do things really, really well. But when we do do something really, really well, it can feel like time almost stands still. With more such moments in our lives, maybe the hours would not run away from us so awfully quickly.

What happens if we adopt the attitude that life is long? Is it so bad to lean back in your office chair for a moment, or take time out when the stresses of life are at their peak? Does everything have to be done at once? Do you really have to check social media every second? Does it matter if you become the best in the world in eight years instead of seven?

Going by the notion that life is short, I would not even have chosen to take up a sport at the age of 23 in the first place. I also would not have spent those countless hours at dark shooting ranges, and I would not have stuck by my goal after those first few years of loss after loss and what was in fact quite a dismal life. If life had been short, I would have made a different choice. I would not have had the courage to set aside anything unrelated to the path towards my vision. I also would not have dared to only fire five shots when a whole day of training was available to me. But because my life is long, or at least it has been so far, I have all the time in the world to set priorities and stick to what I have chosen to focus on. Looking at life like this is not easy in these modern times. It takes a real effort to turn the concept of "time" through 180 degrees. Time and the transitory nature of life can also be thrown into a new light when we suffer an accident or an illness. But even without experience of life's transitory nature, people who avoid accidents and illnesses also seem to interpret life as short, for some reason. The notion that time goes quickly and that life is short thus appears to be a *perception* of time, and of what needs to be done when we have time, rather than what actually happens in that time. Perhaps this feeling is more common in the 21st century than it was in the past? Despite the fact that in our part of the world we are living much longer than we did. It should therefore be possible to change our perception of time, at least on an individual basis, and ideally also on a sociocultural level.

Think how terribly rare it is for us to decide what we should focus on most and then actually do it. Instead, our thoughts often get bogged down in all the things that need to be done before that, and so time runs away from us. Or we try to do all sorts of different things at the same time. Our true focus gets shattered into a thousand small obligations that in no way steer us in the right direction.

Finding time is thus not about prioritising but about *de-prioritising*. And just how easy is that!? asks the prosecutor who has 40 criminal investigations on the go at once, for example. It is not easy, and there are no shortcuts. But processing thoughts about all this also takes up time, not just the work itself. The focus model showed that distracting thoughts are the main culprit in taking up time. These are the thoughts, above all others, that need to be removed, the distracting thoughts about how to find the time for everything that needs to be done.

From an everyday perspective, this is actually quite small beer. Start practising by listening to a colleague when she gives a presentation, for example, and *don't* sit looking at your mobile phone under the table, just pretending to be paying attention. If you have young children – watch them playing in the park, rather than looking at your phone.

Instead of writing a to-do list for the week, try taking some quiet time to sit and work out what it is that you *don't* have to do. Once you have given this some thought, and perhaps mulled it over more than once, you will find that there is actually quite a lot. Maybe you don't have to do that decorating, go to Thailand on holiday or attend that skills development course. Maybe you don't have to do the laundry, clean or answer those e-mails today. Maybe you don't need to go to all the meetings. Maybe you don't even need to train! Now you can write a to-not-do list instead. And gradually all those time-consuming thoughts about everything that "has to be done" will fade away. Time will be freed up, the days will be longer and the conditions for focusing on one thing and doing it well will improve.

Since we are so keen to fill our time, might it be that we are now useless at doing nothing, which in turn makes us useless at having a dull time? Are we so addicted to stimuli and challenge that we have practically forgotten the pleasures of boredom? As a shooter, you get very good at this and, believe me, it is a definite advantage to be well trained in the art of not having fun. Shooters train alone for hours at a time, staring at a target day after day, with the single objective of getting a medal in a sport of which the general public is blissfully unaware. Remarkably, creative solutions often arise out of this necessary perseverance and the associated dullness. Partly in an attempt to make what one is doing just a little more interesting or more challenging, and partly to increase focus. Be patient and the brain will find a solution. It does so because it is in our nature to seek stimulation.

One Easter Saturday during my officer training, I stood alone on the cold, grey indoor shooting range in Halmstad. The range is housed in a red wooden building with a gravel courtyard a few kilometres from the town, and I spent most of my time before lessons, during lunch and after lessons in this shed. There was nothing wrong with the place in itself. Like many other shooting ranges, it was just terribly dull. Sometimes I stood outside for a moment before going in. I used to breathe in the fresh air and drink in a minute or two of the light that I then would not see again for several hours, even in the middle of the lightest summer. It is just so damn ugly, I thought, as I stood looking at this big red lump of a building. In reality, it wasn't really all that ugly, it was just an ordinary red shed in a military area. Ugly, or rather uninviting, is how I felt about the coming isolation and discipline that awaited me inside. Sportspeople often describe their memories of training facilities as "the smell of sweat and camaraderie". This smelled of lead and loneliness.

On this particular evening the loneliness and the cold were particularly raw, probably because it was Easter and all my friends were out on the town celebrating. I remained disciplined and so of course I was going to train all night long. After a while, shot after shot alone created a routine behaviour that was inconsistent with millimetre precision. My concentration was not what it should have been, and standing there shooting without that focus, even if I hit 10s, would have been utterly meaningless. This time, since it was Easter, I decided to let my hair down a bit, take a break and get something to eat.

In my pursuit of food, I found myself cycling past a fancy dress shop and I saw a brightly coloured chicken costume in the window. Completely on impulse, I breezed in and bought a comb, a feathered suit and a beak. Back at the range, I then danced with great abandon in the hall. Finally, I returned to my training, but dressed in my new outfit. The chicken comb, which was front-heavy, had to be correctly balanced and the beak had to be adjusted to accommodate the diopter. My technique was slightly off, but...the very idea that the caretaker or a fellow officer could come in and see Christina Bengtsson, current Swedish champion, dressed as a chicken!

I had so much fun in my solitude that I was almost bursting with laughter internally. Joy coursed through me and suddenly I didn't want to be anywhere else but here on my own in this chilly shed. I recalled every detail of every shot, and I still do. The melancholy was replaced by focus.

But why was my concentration better as a chicken? The main explanation is the balance between challenge and ability. As the ability to do a task increases, bigger challenges are required to achieve a focused state or a good flow. If the task feels overwhelming – the challenge exceeds one's ability – a sense of inadequacy and anxiety arises and that is a poor state in which to achieve focus. Too easy a challenge in relation to ability, on the other hand, creates melancholy and tedium. This was what initially happened in the chicken story. Nothing was challenging me and I was doing the same thing over and over again, nothing was at stake, no-one valued my work, my 10s or my efforts. No-one saw my commitment and no-one was going to ask about it the next day. The environment was dark and bleak, and of course I would rather have been out on the town than doing shooting practice away from all my friends. One way to regain the focus in this drudgery was to up the challenge a little by wearing a chicken comb. It was definitely a bit harder to keep the rifle still. And this impulsive choice also raised my mood to a whole new level.

For many people, handling the drudgery is a greater issue in the context of focus than the problem of the challenge exceeding one's ability. This is not particularly surprising, considering all the experience and trials most of us actually encounter in life and learn to handle. It is therefore important to be able to find focus during periods of boredom. In most cases, including this chicken anecdote, the task – the actual challenge – is not easy to change and maybe it shouldn't be changed. You simply have to embrace the drudgery and let the brain come up with ideas and little moments of madness that break the pattern and, as the chicken did, make the dull task more fun by raising the mood. This shifts the focus from thoughts about "everything else", particularly how incredibly boring the task is, to what is happening now in this moment. Think of the times when you had work to do that required some brainpower and you were trying to focus in a state of irritation or frustration. You'll remember how impossible this is. Focusing on mentally demanding work is about being motivated, pleased and happy. Sometimes our system needs just a little help along the way. Here, a better mood is like the autumn leaf in the World Championship final, a neutral, pleasant thought that knocks out all other distracting thoughts. Or everyday thoughts about the future that constantly remind us what shopping needs to be done or calls need to be made before the end of the day. The task is still being done, but now with a little more comfort, presence and enjoyment, and that is not something to be dismissed. Research shows that a positive mood increases our capacity to think flexibly and follow complex thought processes, which makes it easier to find solutions to problems, both intellectual and personal. Daniel Goleman exemplifies this in his book *Emotional Intelligence*, stating that one way to help someone think through a problem properly is to tell a funny story. Laughter and high spirits are thought to help free up our thoughts and associations, allowing us to spot connections that we otherwise would have missed. According to Goleman, this mental competence is important not only for creativity, but also in unpicking complex correlations. In her book *Mindfulness i hjärnan (Mindfulness in the Brain)*, Åsa Nilsonne writes that positive emotions make us think more globally, while negative emotions lead us into a more restricted view of the situation. It is thus highly desirable to have fun and be in the right frame of mind for what we're doing, as this gives a major boost to our chances of achieving focus.

Might this be the reason why we fill our time with new challenges and projects, and like to have several balls in the air – to avoid boredom and melancholy? Instead of doing one thing, one project at a time, and giving it our full attention? Is it just too dull or too difficult to maintain focus? It is clearly better to have many irons in the fire and be happy, alert and sharp in all contexts, than to wrestle, in sadness and gloom, with one thing and not even do that well. But having so much going on that you and your life feel splintered also gets you nowhere. There are actually only two ways to meet the brain's need for challenge and stimulation. Either you stop doing the boring task and move on to another one, or you settle into the boring task, allow your brain to find creative and ingenious solutions and regain your focus.

Let us test the notion of managing to prioritise and do only the most important thing, despite the risk of boredom, and to stick with this, to the exclusion of almost everything else. Can the chicken anecdote be of any use in this context?

Well the answer is *yes, it can.* Obviously, there is an issue with the anecdote that is difficult for us, and an absolute impossibility for our leading figures in society, no matter how funny it would be, and that is dressing up in public. Trust in the head of a bank, a fashion house or a multinational would crumble, according to our current social norms, if they wore a chicken comb on their head in the boardroom, on the red carpet or on the speaker's podium. It is enough, in this case, to understand the principle at least. Then each individual is free to experiment however they wish without revealing themselves to the outside world. An enterprising student I spoke to a while ago considered the idea of dressing up in a suit and tie at home to improve his focus in front of the computer. Another tip, for example at a meeting or conference that has become almost unbearably dull and boring, is to imagine the other people in the room as different animals. Suddenly it becomes quite interesting to imagine the modest keynote speaker as a giraffe at the podium. See the political expert as an impatient little beaver off to one side, busily taking notes, as the bespectacled mole next to her mutters to himself. To begin with, these fantasies can seem silly and shameful, but no-one will ever know about them except you. And that is what is so amusing. This is a trick I used to employ in the many briefing rooms in the Armed Forces, where orders are given and decisions are supposed to be made. Despite the brain seeing something different to what it should be seeing, it becomes sharper and the mood improves its performance. Conversely, it is quite liberating, when I'm standing in front of a collection of uniformed decision-makers, to see them as a flock of animals. This image makes the situation less intimidating, taking the edge off any doubts I might have about their interest in my message, or concerns about the opinion of a superior or upcoming comments about my conduct. If I place them all in a group of regular penguins in front of me, the situation becomes less threatening and my focus ends up not on their critical facial expressions, but on a pleasant and neutral state. "Reimagining" the environment like this thus has an effect in moments of both boredom and performance.

I made use of this reimagining ahead of shooting finals in front of an audience. That period behind the scenes with all the other finalists, before it was time to walk out in front of the public and take my place in my lane, was always a hugely nervous time. It was also so irritating that, having fought so hard and managed to reach the final, I now suddenly wanted to run away as quickly as I could. So contradictory and so stupid! I used to stand there, wondering why on earth I had chosen to subject myself to such unpleasantness. The situation was sometimes so alarming that my hands shook, and not getting this shaking under control would condemn me to failure. Starting a final with shaky hands had happened before, and it couldn't happen again.

As I stepped out into the spotlight and headed towards my lane, I imagined the audience as a herd of animals to whom I was happy to reveal my nervousness. I turned towards the herd and cheerfully waved a trembling hand. I smiled at the whole spectacle and the madness of being part of it. And as soon as I revealed my nerves, they began to drain from me.

The final then became more like a show at a zoo (not a show for people, but for animals, so a human zoo I suppose). The animals had come here to watch us finalists, us nervous humans who were now going to try and stand as still as possible and hit a target ten times in a row. This idea alone provided a welcome distance from the challenge and the unpleasant seriousness of it all. Now the moment had been rendered sufficiently harmonious (and comical), and I was in the right mood to complete my task in the spotlight.

Don't Set Your Sights on
too Much

The focus model is based on our ability to think forwards and backwards in time. So far I have largely talked about freeing ourselves from distracting thoughts of the past or the future, either in a performance situation or in a state of relaxed focus. But thinking backwards and forwards in time is also of great value to us humans. It is this capacity that makes us so constructive and creative. This capacity combines with our language to offer us quite singular opportunities. The future is in our hands in a way that sets us clearly apart from other animals, exactly because we know that it exists and can reflect, fantasise and talk and dream about it. This also brings with it a certain responsibility, a responsibility to make best use of this capacity that we possess, and to think as good thoughts as possible. We should be grateful for the ability to think in this way, even though this gift is also a cause of brooding and anxiety, and one that often disrupts our focus. As we know, thoughts about the future have a direct impact on the present, but thinking about the future is not in itself a worry – on the contrary. The key issue is *what* we think about it

In autumn 2003, the European Championships were about to land on home turf. 625 competitors from 46 nations, many of them among the world's elite, would be descending on the Scandinavium arena in Gothenburg for a whole week of shooting. Organising an international competition locally is not something the Swedish Sport Shooting Association does very often. Expectations and levels of enthusiasm were high.

Between the organised training camps, I spent countless hours training on my own as usual.

At the Morup shooting range, you had to turn a handle to move the target backwards and forwards. If I wound the handle too fast, there was a risk that the target holder would spin round with such force that the target would come flying off. I cranked away until I had blisters on my hands, I slept in the shower room and my mother brought me egg sandwiches because I forgot to eat. Instead of food, I sustained myself on my picture of future success at the European Championships.

I arranged my own training camps and Roger came along to practise shooting in the final. I may have failed to make the final at the last World Cup, as usual, but I had squirreled away images from the final as seen from the stands – the presentation of the finalists, the applause, the countdown, followed by the silence of the crowd, a nervous cough from the stands ... the sharp crack of eight shots, and finally the jubilant roar from a thrilled audience.

Roger and I shot final after final during our training camps and fantasised about the setting for the final at Skandinavium, and what it would feel like to step up onto the winners' podium in front of a home crowd. I imagined who in the audience would roar when I hit the deciding 10 on the final shot that would put my name and Sweden top of the leader board.

In Gothenburg the excitement was building day by day. The team managers had high hopes and the preparations went beyond anything I'd experienced before. As a shooter, I'd never stayed in such a smart hotel.

The day before the big match arrived and all the preparations were done. Despite all the perfectionism and meticulous training, technical, physical and mental, the reality remained – the margins were still just as tight, the competitors just as skilled and the 10 just as small.

The excitement and the pressure continued to build all through the day. In a subtle way, the whole team began to tense up, and irrelevant details took on more and more importance. I myself started coming up with concerns that I shared with my coach, who for safety's sake took them seriously. We became serious and careful, testing the rifle's air pressure, checking the ammunition's muzzle velocity and photographing the shooting lanes to mentally prepare for the light and the surroundings – just to be sure. The fact that I was not more confident after these serious tests and preparations, combined with my teammates complaints that they had slept badly in their beds, gave me pause for thought – how on earth could a complaint about the hotel's beds have cropped up? We shooters, who are used to military barracks in the Czech Republic, Sävsjö and Skövde, and who ahead of the European Championships had slept on the floor and wound the targets in Morup, were now sleeping in a fancy hotel! Suddenly we were expressing needs we never knew existed before, and ones that in all likelihood would not have the slightest effect on the next day's performance. Everyone knew this, the coaches and the competitors, but subconsciously there was a comfort in having something to blame in the event that it all went down the tubes the next day.

Tomorrow felt overwhelming. We were under pressure. What more could be done when everything was perfect?

So how could we feel under such terrible pressure about something for which we were so well prepared? We had pictured ourselves performing at our peak. Pictured ourselves in the final and on the podium. According to classic sports psychology, visualisation is vital in achieving set goals. Seeing yourself as winning, succeeding, achieving what you want or what has to be completed within the framework of a particular task has proven to be highly effective. In so doing, when it comes to your time to perform, you are familiar with the situation, and can almost automatically complete your performance as if your body was pre-programmed. You feel as if you "have been here before" and the situation therefore holds no fears.

But it is worth noting that visualising yourself on top of the podium has the greatest impact if you also have a strong *conviction* that you will get there deeply rooted in your inner soul. Any doubt, no matter how small, about the positive visualisation of your goal can upset everything. There is nothing wrong with doubt itself. It is a healthy critical faculty that should not be dismissed out of hand. It should be given the necessary space and allowed to be a piece in the game. Doubt can take time to erase and to work through. A goal on the other hand is easier to change.

Ahead of the European Championships in Gothenburg, however, there was no appetite for that. The bar had been set unusually high. And everyone stuck with it, despite the doubts being so strong that irrelevant details started being blamed in a perfectly prepared world. This slightly overambitious goal played on everyone's minds, and as the big day approached, it grew into an unpleasant expectation that nobody really believed was achievable. The level of expectation fed our doubts, which grew and grew. It didn't matter how much we visualised, in fact that just seemed to make things worse.

Imagine a timeline on which a goal for the future has been placed in the form of a podium right at one end – the symbol of success. Imagine yourself, or something you dream will come true, on top of this podium, drawn for example as an overjoyed stick figure. Create a symbol for your success, your dream. The starting point for this picture is the importance of setting up goals for yourself or for your business, and the importance of seeing yourself or your business succeed in the future.

Creating internal visualisations of your goals and expressing these, not just to yourself but also to others, is a precondition for moving forward, motivating yourself and others, and keeping yourself on track. This exemplifies the best side of our capacity to think "forwards". Goals are there to create drive and motivation and to serve as beacons for navigating life. Let us accept this argument as fundamental, before we carry on with the next.

Assuming now that a visualisation of the goal has been created and that the drive towards this has been set in motion – is this visualisation entirely risk-free? Is it guaranteed that the goal will be achieved because of this mental picture?

Apparently not. It certainly didn't work at the European Championships in Gothenburg. Consider how many people say they are going to achieve this or that, and see themselves winning, but never do. This mass of people is rarely talked about. It requires so much more than setting up goals and visualising them to actually achieve them.

Sport is the clearest of examples. Think how many people have set a goal of winning at a World Championship or Olympic Games when we all know that only one person can take that gold medal. We are impressed by the goal-oriented focus of the person who won. We decide that the goal of winning is a must. Visualizing ourselves to succeed has become a truth, as if success would otherwise not be possible. But what about all the others, those who didn't win? They all had the same visualisation but failed to win – so is that visualisation really such a critical success factor? Did everyone who saw themselves topping the podium visualise the correct goal that matched their capabilities? Or, when it came down to it, was it a source of anxiety and distraction?

It is perhaps a little odd that we so readily set goals for ourselves, often without giving a moment's thought to the effect they have on our focus – the one factor above all else that might determine whether we actually achieve our desires.

Yes, I accept the importance of visualising goals, but having the courage to change them is at least as important. Once again, it is important to take note of what you are thinking, and why you are thinking that way. Is the visualisation a personal desire, or is it an external expectation? Do you have doubts? Does the visualisation match your actual capabilities? What effect does this visualisation have on you? *Why* do you have it? Is it absolutely necessary? Has the desire to win been balanced with the acceptance of losing? Has the visualisation developed into an overwhelming expectation, or such a foregone conclusion that it is no longer a challenge?

Above all: is the need to feed your ego and be recognised – to receive external validation – the driving force rather than a genuine desire and belief in yourself and your abilities?

In simple terms, the target being visualised will fall into one of three categories:

1. A goal driven by external validation
2. A goal set on the basis of external expectation
3. A goal rooted in your inner core as a genuine conviction

Most of us encounter these different types of goals at some point. Of course, the latter option is preferable, but we can't always demand this absolute purity from ourselves. The world changes and we change with it. We are governed by different needs as things change around us. What we *can* do, however, is carefully take note of *what* governs us, what the driving force really is, so that we can revise the goal we have visualised and focus our thoughts. For example, a goal that plays to our need for external validation has a major impact on our drive, which may be a good thing, but it is more likely to lead to eternal pursuit than to concrete success. Similarly, a goal that has been set because it is *expected* by outsiders is rarely associated with runaway success.

When genuine goals are visualised, by which I mean goals clearly related to actual capabilities, and when the drive to achieve them is securely rooted in a genuine desire and belief, there are no obvious obstacles to success. What can often put a spanner in the works is having too strong a desire to achieve the goal. In addition to the demands that creep in as the moment of the expected success approaches, there is a risk that any focus on what does and does not have to be done along the way might be lost. If, in a competition situation, you start becoming interested in beating your opponent or securing a valuable professional contract, the competition risks becoming a distraction rather than an opportunity to focus on what is happening. Putting in the necessary work and allowing yourself to listen openly to internal and external influences, on the road towards your goal, is thus a factor. Your *attitude* to a goal and the way you *act* on your way towards it is therefore at least as important as the goal itself. This requires focus on the present and is a bit easier to manage when a genuine goal has been visualised.

A genuine goal takes hold inside, both emotionally and intellectually. A goal that has gained an emotional foothold will not easily be forgotten, that's for sure. And so there don't need to be reminders about it every day either, not to ourselves, to managers, leaders or employees. Trying to encourage the people around you towards ambitious goals is often more a waste of time and energy than it is productive. This is as true individually as it is professionally and privately. There is no need to worry about losing motivation and drive once a genuine goal has been established. Constantly reminding yourself about towards where you are aiming and constantly seeing yourself at your "destination" in fact constantly shifts your focus from what is happening in the present to what may happen in the future, and that is not particularly helpful. After all, it is *now* that the situation needs analysing, it is *now* that any doubts need to be identified and it is *now* that the work needs to be done – with as much focus as possible. This becomes difficult if your thoughts are always jumping forwards in time.

The smart thing to do instead is to clear the visualised goal from your mind. Why? To ensure better focus on what is happening and needs to be done here and now, and to free yourself from demands as you knuckle down to the tough job at hand. Focusing on your work towards your goal is not about visualising and reminding yourself of your goal. This directs your thoughts to the future, not the present. It is more about focusing your mind on the job that needs doing now, and doing it well. It is about being free from pressure and the demands that thoughts about a visualised goal often compound. Freeing your mind from the goal also improves your ability to be open and receptive to signals and changes in yourself and the world around you.

This was overlooked by the Swedish team in the lead-up to the European Championships in Gothenburg. This whole story reveals too great a focus on the goal and too little focus on the actual truth of the matter: that on this occasion we were actually a number of places away from the best in Europe. All our final preparations were based on thoughts about the future, without even noticing that they were making us anxious. Roger and I visualised and saw ourselves shining both in the finals and on the winners' podium. Much of our training was channelled into "reaching the final and getting a medal". We were entirely unaware that the goal driving us was not our own, and not genuinely rooted in our own self-belief. Instead of focusing on the now, and being open, self-aware and realistic, we were unwittingly trapped by the overwhelming demands of our visualised goal.

The consequence was that going into the final days, we well equipped and well prepared Swedes had such a lack of confidence that we were already looking for excuses of any kind, even the hotel beds. We blamed whatever we could, in case we failed to achieve the goal of medals on our home turf – a back-up excuse in case it all went wrong. The first and simplest indication that a goal is doing more harm than good is when you or those around you begin to seize on anything as the reason why the desired outcome was not achieved, or why something went as badly as it did. There is nothing to suggest that successful individuals or successful companies are blessed with more luck than anyone else. However, it has been shown that those who rarely succeed often blame bad luck.

Sometimes it goes so far that the bad luck becomes a goal in itself. In shooting, where the margins are so incredibly small, it is very tempting to take this approach. How many times during my career have I heard myself, my competitors or my colleagues describe an unsuccessful match with the words "it actually went really well, I was just unlucky to end up with eight 9.9s," i.e. eight 9s a mere tenth of a millimetre outside the 10. The results monitor shows points with decimals, but these are not counted in the initial rounds. At that stage you just get a 9 or a 10. Nevertheless, our minds were keen to point out that these 9.9s brought us "so close" to the final, a medal or a world record. Instead of accepting the fact, during the course of the match, that a 9 had been shot, the opportunity is created to have something to blame in the event that things don't work out. This train of thought is unable to make headway in a focused mind; it can only take hold in mind that is afraid of not reaching the set goal. And such thoughts naturally give rise to even more 9.9s. When the goal is then not achieved, bad luck can be blamed and the match can be left with a false sense of honour intact.

Let me make a reference to love here. When love enters our life and we want it to stay, how many of us haven't painted a rosy picture of how our life is going to pan out? Everyday worries and you own and your new partner's shortcomings are blown away by a future image of a successful relationship. The image of a happy life where you are loved and fault-free brings a moment of brightness to an otherwise grey and humdrum existence and we stand by the belief that everything is going to work out. This is all well and good. But what happens when it becomes apparent that real life, and indeed you and your partner, don't fit the imagined image?

It is hard for you and for others to accept that you are not the happy and fault-free person in the image. When your relationship and life don't turn out as expected, it is easy to see yourself as faultless when it comes to this visualised goal and simply blame external circumstances. This is an easier approach than adjusting the image based on a realisation of who you actually are. Regrettably, the onus often falls on other people, who have to carry the blame that actually belongs to you. Just like with the 9.9s, finding reasons to blame someone else becomes a goal in itself.

The struggle for a successful relationship is often accompanied by a refusal to see yourself and your nearest and dearest in the *true* light of the present. You would rather just see everything in the *desired* light of the future. This takes away the capacity to be happy and grateful for what you have now. Missing out on gratefulness for what *is*, and for what you *have*, is absolutely the weakest link in the chain that we call life, about which we have such grand thoughts. Gratefulness pales into insignificance as the mind constantly chases after all the things that have yet to be achieved, and this can easily tarnish any love you might have for yourself, your partner or your current situation.

The capacity to be grateful is backed up by the capacity for focus. It is difficult for the brain to be grateful while striving to achieve a future that is so different from the present.

Today there is plenty of talk about self-image and how important it is to look at yourself with a positive eye. There is nothing wrong with that, but have we considered that our image of ourself is usually bound up with a *future* image? An image of where you are going and what you intend to achieve and become. It is not surprising that our self-image works in this way – the only way the brain has to create an image of something is to put together a kind of photofit from stored memories. Without memory, there is no way to create an image of the past, present or future. So self-image is based on memories that the brain has cleverly put together to create an image of who we are today and who we want to be. All the building blocks for these images are thus in the memory. It is interesting to note there that the brain has a tendency to selectively forget failures. Instead, it recasts the memory in a more favourable light. This is why our self-image tends to be quite good, sometimes perhaps too good. It is therefore worth occasionally thinking about just how well this image fits with reality. A little self-examination now and then serves a good purpose.

It makes it easier to feel grateful and to accept your own shortcomings, as well as those of the people close to you. It is about critically examining, on a cognitive level, who you are now, and being able to clearly distinguish between the true image of the moment and the image of a desired future.

A future vision or dream is no bad thing as long it is clearly separated from the so-called "hard facts" about what you are like, what you can do and what you have right now. Enjoying a temporary trip into the world of fantasy and dreams about success is, of course, a good thing. But it requires an anchor point, a focus on who we are and what we have here and now. Without this focus, our thoughts will always skip to the wonderful image we have created for ourselves. Obviously they are happier lingering there than in the present, particularly if that present is rather grey and sad, and so we become disappointed in reality.

Could it be that a constant reminder of a rose-tinted future vision makes the present day feel even greyer and sadder than it actually is? That doubts about who you are today might strike more readily if an image of what you *will* achieve or *will* become is ever-present? It is particularly painful when the cold hard facts highlight just how far from the imagined future you actually are, and doubts about getting there have begun to eat away at you. People who strongly identify with their future vision and who have goals such as training more, becoming healthier and slimmer, are recommended not to read health magazines or look at themselves in the mirror for a while. Otherwise, the disappointment will be too great and hopelessness will replace belief, discipline and stamina. Constantly suffering disappointment when reality fails to live up to the future vision has a destructive effect.

It would be better to draw a line through this rose-tinted image for a while and learn to love and live with the image in the mirror right now. This is the image on which the hard work should be based, not the idealised image, whether of individuals or relationships.

Knowing with any certainty whether your future vision is knocking you out of focus in a destructive way is not easy. Even in the face of clear indications that the vision is beyond our actual capabilities, resources or strength, we prefer to grimly hold on to the goal we once set ourselves. It's as if we are ashamed of surrendering to the fact that the vision needs changing, instead of being proud of the skill involved in making a sound assessment of the current situation.

So what can you do to get a better grip on whether your goal is helping or hindering?

As we've seen, one concrete early warning sign comes in the form of the blame game. Taking note of *how* you think or express yourself is another, for example in your relationship, in the mirror, in your training or in your work. What are your thoughts telling you, during training for that golf tournament, before that essay has to be written or ahead of a coming performance situation? Have you ever found yourself thinking along the lines of:

This is going really badly! I'm so rubbish at this!
This isn't going to end well! How will this work?

The first two sentences contain the phrase *is going* and *I am*. Note that this is the present tense and describes how something is going right now. The fact that what you're training for or working on is going badly should not be seen as a negative thought that hinders you on your way to your goal. It is healthy and realistic thinking. A self-examination that should be given free rein.

Worrying that things are not going to go well or wondering how everything will go are, however, in the future tense. This "future-tense thinking" reveals that your thoughts are stuck in a future time and on a future goal, rather than the present reality. What you are doing now is being compared with a future image. Anxiety has crept in, or life is lived in constant pursuit of a goal that is in fact pure wishful thinking.

So what happens if we erase it?

Think back to the timeline with a podium, the image of success, at the far end. Take the podium away! Rub it out or put a cross through it! All that is left is a line. Initially, it will feel empty and perhaps a little meaningless. Alarming even. This is because it pushes against what we are used to and against our identity. We often think so much about a goal in front of us that it becomes part of our very being. We identify ourselves with the image of future success and actually feel both naked and small without it. To start with, we lose a degree of pride, particularly if the goal has been something that has fed our external satisfaction.

But once this immediate emptiness has settled, something happens. What happens is that your thoughts focus fully on the present, not on things to come. The mind focus on what is important right now, and the scope to find moments of relaxed focus on the way towards the goal also increases. We find it easier to feel grateful. Chance and creativity are more often embraced automatically, and focus levels at work rise. Attempts to find things to blame in case everything goes wrong fade away when the goal is erased. Quality asserts itself and you find that you don't have to train or work like crazy "just in case".

Visualisation is thus sometimes capable of disrupting our focused work on achieving our goal, and this is something we need to look out for. If there is the slightest doubt or feeling of anxiety associated with thoughts about the goal, the recommended course of action is either to change the goal or to erase it entirely for the time being. Ignoring the visualisation for a moment is not as cavalier as it sounds. In fact, it makes good sense. Only then can the right focus be achieved and the true image of the capabilities and the possibilities available to us – the cold hard facts – be embraced.

One way for us shooters to practise freeing ourselves from our visualisations is to be disciplined and not look at the results during training. Shot after shot is fired in as concentrated and perfect a way as possible, but with a T-shirt or towel draped over the adjacent results monitor. The purpose of this is to practise never placing your focus on the results and the points total, but just, shot after shot, hour after hour, to focus your attention on performing properly. Initially, this is a fairly boring exercise. But it is very rewarding. If, in your mind, you translate a shooting match of 60 shots over the course of around two hours into what you need to get done before your break, into today's target at work, into a long-term project, into parenting or into your life, my point becomes more tangible: focus on the here and now.

In some contexts, however, erasing the visualisation is not so simple. Sometimes, we stand there with an expectation hanging over us and have no choice but to do the best we can. Even though it would be best for a sportsperson, for example, to reveal in an interview the day before a championship: "There'll be no medal today," or for a minister to say, the day before a key global summit: "I don't think we're going to get an agreement," it can seem somehow inappropriate. Often some other person has set up the goal with which we are uncomfortable and in which we find ourselves. So what can we do?

Let us return to the day before the big day at the European Championships in the Skandinavium stadium. I was sick with nerves, and almost hoped that I might sprain my foot on the steps to the breakfast room, so I would have a reason to avoid enduring this fiasco. Everything was perfect.

And yet the next day was overwhelming. The whole team was under pressure and I wondered what more could be done, when everything was so perfectly prepared? What should I do? Something had to be done. The pattern needed to be broken, thoughts banished, but how? How could I do it? The idea of going from faultless to fool was inspired.

I headed off to my parents to pick up some old jeans, a studded belt, a black wig, a headband and an old microphone. I got Roger involved and with a view to "lightening the mood the day before the match" I asked the team manager whether I could perform a ten-minute show during the evening gathering. My request was granted and three hours later, dressed as a rock star, I climbed up onto a makeshift stage in front of my fellow shooters, the national team managers and the odd suited Olympic Committee member. Roger served as my roadie, handing me props and, on my command, he pressed play on the tape recorder to get the show started.

Singing solo in front of a crowd was one of the most uncomfortable things I could imagine. Now I had compelled myself to slide across the stage, to the beat of the music, like Axl Rose in Guns n' Roses and belt out *Sweet Child o' Mine* from the heart for friends and strangers alike. I was incredibly nervous. The sweat poured off me and my legs were shaking. It was acutely embarrassing, but so much fun.

I saw astonished faces, camera flashes and jaws dropped to people's knees. It no doubt sounded terrible, but the show was a success, the laughter relieved the tension and thoughts about the next day's match were swept away just for a moment.

We laughed so much! The national team managers maybe thought it was all a bit wild the day before a match, but in my world I knew: stepping out onto the range the next day was no longer a worry. Taking part in a European Championship on home turf was no longer overwhelming. I had been training for it for many years, so compared with that evening's performance, it was a piece of cake.

I didn't become European champion, but I did shoot a personal best, I was the top Swede and I had learnt the art of lowering expectations and not staring blindly at the goal.

What basically happened here was that the brain got some much-needed rest in an otherwise high-pressure situation. And that rest was achieved by "erasing" the visualised goal for the next day's dreadful match, just for a moment. This provided the space for a liberating and lighter mood to take over. Creative new solutions were created in that moment. Focus on a new task helped the brain to discard worrying thoughts about the future and the goal. Relaxed focus achieved. The fact that the show established some real distance from the next day's task and made it seem much easier in comparison was a splendid bonus.

This way of handling "the day before the big day" became an established part of my modus operandi. I didn't get up and sing before every championship, but I did do similarly crazy things. Many saw it as rather flippant. But whatever was at stake, the things I did had an exceedingly serious purpose. What I do to get myself, and hopefully those around me, to "switch off" varies, but it always has the same effect on my mind. It doesn't usually have to be particularly remarkable, and it's better, of course, if those around you are along for the ride.

It is exactly when we believe we should be most proper and think most about our important goal that we should instead have the courage and freedom to chill out and let ourselves go on a mental level. How you do this is entirely up to you. The main thing is to cut that strong tie to the future goal for a moment, so the mind can access a different train of thought rather than constantly pursuing perfectionism and faultlessness.

Even when you know that the goal is genuine, reasonable and a positive driver, and not overwhelming, there is one variant that favours the achievement of focus. If we are locked onto a visualised goal, we can now choose to break through and past it instead with another goal further on in the future. But a goal of a very different nature. Let me take an example: Roger and I are focusing on the World Cup in Milan a few months down the line. We're finding it hard to think about anything else. We both want a place on the podium to qualify for a place at the Olympics. This is a reasonable goal. Yet there is still a risk that we will be overtaken by such a strong desire to achieve that goal that we will drift towards a more unreasonable image painted by the brain, which will put us under acute pressure in the lead-up to the World Cup or once we're actually shooting in Milan. The visualisation becomes so detailed, explicit and debated that eventually nothing else exists.

In an everyday context, this is often referred to as being extremely goal-oriented and extremely focused. But I would delete the word "focused" in that sentence. Goal-oriented, yes. But not focused, at least not on the right thing. The visualisation now takes up so much space in our minds that life after the World Cup has faded almost out of existence. That is not sensible. That is to be obsessed. It can cause a lack of focus just when we need that focus most. It can cause unwarranted anxiety – the goal takes on too big a role in life and becomes equated with your very existence. To get us through this situation, Roger and I coined the phrase: "Is there life after WC?" We asked ourselves this question one day when we noticed that our thoughts all went as far as the goal at the World Cup, and after that there was nothing. To answer "yes" to this almost existential question, we had to formulate and visualise another goal. In contrast to the other one, it could be entirely free from expectation. It just had to lodge an image in the brain that nibbled away a little at the edges of the main goal. An image to remind us that life will go on after that main goal. That is the sole purpose of the new goal. The key here is to take the brain's capacity to think forwards in time and play with it in a smart way. We created a goal and visualised it in the same detail that we had devoted to the image of us on the World Cup shooting range. Our new visualised image was of us having ice cream together by a fountain after the World Cup. And that ice cream by a fountain would happen – and here is the point – *no matter how* the matches went for us. Win or lose, and irrespective of whether one of us would be eating ice cream as a champion and the other as a loser, the ice cream would be enjoyed to the full. The new goal told us that there was life after the World Cup and placed a blanket of calm over the otherwise increasingly expectation-filled image of success.

Now we could happily concentrate on our hopes and desires and keep our nerves under control.

In this chapter, we have seen that one's focus can actually increase if the visualised goal is erased, particularly if the goal is set by other people or is driven by a need for external validation. Breaking up an expected pattern of perfection and faultlessness and doing the odd crazy thing before a demand-laden goal helps. If the goal is backed up by genuine conviction, but one's focus on what needs to be done properly here and now gets derailed, a new, fun little goal for further on in the future can be a good strategy for regaining that focus.

But this all begs the question: why do we have big goals anyway? Where do they come from and how can we remain strong when we don't achieve them?

Suggested addition:
"By erasing the picture of a future goal , focus lays on what we are and what we have, instead of chasing after what we are not and don´t have".

Our Inner Core

In this chapter, we will take a more in-depth look at our goals and our dreams, how they come into being and where they come from. How should we approach them in a healthy and constructive manner? Do they benefit anyone other than ourselves? What happens if we don't achieve our goal? How strongly do we identify with it?

Why is it so hard to see what we already have and are? What's the secret of being able to aim for new and better things while also being satisfied with things as they are?

No matter where in the world we come from, getting angry and offended if our progress towards a personal goal is impeded is a natural reaction. However, the actual consequences of what happens when this goal is achieved or not achieved depend largely on who we are and where in the world we live. Here in this part of the world, we usually already have everything we could wish for. So what are we striving for relative to those who have nothing? What do we actually have to lose if we don't achieve the goals of our dreams?

These questions bring to mind friends around the world that I have met at competitions and training camps. Pistol shooter Alexandr Petriv hails from Lviv in Ukraine, and he and I got our first tastes of major international success at the same time. The first time we spoke was when we were waiting in the "queue" for the winners' podium, where the medallists tend to shake hands and congratulate each other without actually knowing much about each other's performances, feelings or thoughts. We were both extremely happy: two inexperienced winners, caught off-guard by the sense of pride we felt at having medals around our necks. We met in a state of euphoria, and would share our highs and lows together for many years to come. It was in France in 2003 that I had the privilege of winning a European Championship bronze medal, thanks mainly to my team mates at that time. From then on, our paths crossed regularly and – despite Alexandr's limited English – we shared a valued sense of solidarity. When you share the same dreams and both spend much of your lives at shooting ranges, factors such as background and language are not particularly important. We understood each other.

When we met over the years, Alexandr would usually greet me with a cheery "Christina! How's life?" I would reply with a few carefully chosen and easily understood words. When I asked him the same question, he nearly always replied: "Life is good – shooting not so good!" We would laugh and continue our training.

What fascinated me about Alexandr was his attitude. He and I shared the same goals, and were both successful. We both thought that life was treating us extremely well. And yet our backgrounds and lives were completely different.

I remember how I felt when he proudly described his family and how they lived. Despite the language barrier, I could picture them clearly. He lived with his entire family – his parents, his sisters and their children – in just a few square metres. His father was ill with cancer. I felt truly humbled when I thought of his lot in life. At the same time, I also experienced a sense of gratitude – tinged with guilt – for my own situation. I already had everything he dreamed of. As did all my family and friends. And his account of what a World Championship or Olympic gold would mean for him and his nearest and dearest cast my own quest for medals in a new light: It would mean financial security for him and his entire family. What kind of incentive did I have compared with what he had told me? Medals would certainly bring me pride, joy and attention, and possibly the odd sponsorship deal, but all this was purely egotistical. Few of those around me would benefit from my success. Proud parents, friends and team managers are all well and good, but from this new perspective my focus suddenly felt a little less admirable. Think of all the many shooters all over the world – and not just shooters, but all the people of the world – who have so little that their goals and dreams are more or less essential. They arise and are needed in order to meet basic needs. From a welfare perspective, their goals and dreams take on a different significance to our own. Alexandr and I shared the same goals, and yet they were different.

Goals can be divided up into two types: those that fulfil a real need for more (more or less essential for survival) and those that fulfil a desire for more (self-fulfilment). I call the first type *essential* goals, since they really do make a difference on a more or less essential level. The second type are what I call *invented* goals, since we don't actually need more than we already have. Here, we can make the link with Abraham Maslow's famous hierarchy of needs, with its six levels or steps. The first four, the "deficiency needs", are mankind's fundamental needs: physiological needs such as food and water, security and safety, love and belonging, and self-esteem. It is only once these needs have been satisfied that people seek self-actualisation, and many of us in the Western world find ourselves on this fifth level. We already have what we need and are striving to fulfil ourselves, develop ourselves, improve ourselves, become more competent, become more beautiful, win praise and be stimulated. But where is Alexandr? Strangely enough, he is also at the upper levels. He even seems to be on the sixth level, which Maslow coined self-transcendence – giving oneself away. Despite the fact that – compared with many other people – he doesn't have everything, he thinks he does. He is therefore driven by a desire to create better conditions, including for people other than himself. So, how is it that some people think they have everything when this isn't actually true, while others don't realise they have everything even though they do?

Essential goals and dreams with purposes that are more focused on basic needs are not particularly common in our part of the world. Here, there is often a peculiar paradox: The more we possess on both a personal and a prosperity level, the greater our desire for more. This is because we all need goals and dreams. Some also have the capacity and the extra energy that I, too, had, but don't know what to do with it. Those of us who already have everything must, quite simply, make up our goals. If we have everything we actually need, our thoughts often don't go much further than "I want even more". If we then fail to pay attention to our inner value, it's easy to give in to all the external influences and all manner of ideals – be more attractive, younger, slimmer, richer, more effective, achieve an even higher status or maybe become world champion. Even having more time and more rest can be a (stressful) goal in itself. Essential goals and dreams are easier in that they appear of their own volition, a form of survival instinct with a worthy purpose. They arise as a need like those on the slightly lower steps of Maslow's hierarchy of needs. On the other hand, they are tougher since the consequences when they are not achieved are harsh. However unpleasant it is to lose or not achieve our wishes, those of us marking time on the self-actualisation step never fall as hard as those who lose a more basic need. There isn't actually any pressure on us, since we can never fall particularly hard. And yet we act as if we've lost everything if we don't succeed. Why do we feel this way?

Our goals are sometimes only a picture of what we don't have, or don't think we have, such as beauty, money, family, success, medals and fame. We focus on what we think we don't have instead of focusing on everything we have. Despite all the good things in our lives, we focus on the fear of not achieving our (invented) goal instead of enjoying what we already have. Worries about not achieving our goal have then trapped us, and our focus is on forward-looking thoughts: Just imagine it... The goal serves to fill an inner void and reminds us what we lack instead of reinforcing what we already have. You might think that if the goal or the dream has been made up by a brain whose owner already has most things, it should be a simple matter of going for it, since life goes on, even if not as envisaged. But despite the fact that there are no actual obstacles and there is no need to worry about failing, it's not always easy to feel this way. The goal applies the brakes instead of flinging the door wide open to life's opportunities. This is because we often identify strongly with our personal goals. Here, we have to ask ourselves why we want to achieve these. How strongly do you identify with this vision of the future, this desire? Identifying too strongly with a personal goal results in the feeling that we've lost a part of ourselves if we don't succeed. We feel as if we've lost something vital, even if this isn't actually true.

I who often felt pressured, and who with my relatively few years of training behind me often felt that I was the underdog, was forced to find a success factor other than my technical proficiency. In a sense, my goals didn't really correspond with the amount of training I'd had. If I thought about my competitors' experience and proficiency compared with my own, I grew nervous and thought that I would never stand a chance. Instead, I needed to see what I had that the others didn't have. I started to look at what I had as a person and what I was – which was actually a great deal. This led me to see my inner strength, and that I didn't have anything vital to lose, regardless of the outcome. This was liberating, audacious and extremely successful.

The thought came to me during a nervous final in Ankara, Turkey. After three weeks of intensive training at the Marksmanship Unit at Fort Benning in the USA, a pretty lousy World Cup in Sydney and a first round that I had barely scraped through, I now found myself among the ranks of the world elite with a chance at success. In front of me were competitors from the great shooting nations: Russia, the USA, Germany, Ukraine and China. The Chinese competitor was closest to me. It was the Chinese that I feared the most. They were so well trained, and in contrast to us Swedes they had been professionals from a very young age, shooting like skilfully programmed robots. Behind them stood a pack of coaches, with their dark clothing and determined gazes.

I was clearly the underdog and was under huge pressure, but I changed my way of thinking.

This skilled shooter in front of me was just as on-edge and anxious as I was. And just think about the incredible pressure *she* was facing, I thought. Her entire continued existence depends on whether she gets a 9 or a 10 – a difference of just a millimetre. Compared to me, shooting is all she has and is probably the only thing that can take her from a life of mediocrity to achieve wealth and success. She has trained hard for this moment, and is at one with her shooting. *I*, on the other hand, am so much more than just shooting. If I get a 9, what happens? Nothing.

I felt such strength in my *inner being*, and a wave of pride washed away my nervous thoughts. My sense of identify lay with who I was and what I already had – in my inner being, and not in having to achieve my goal – a fundamental realisation for both success and life in general.

It was the power of *my inner being* that won the match, not my skill.

Paying attending to, identifying with and recognising one's inner being is what being in focus is all about. I have chosen to call our inner being *our inner core*. This is where we find the secret to being able to focus on new and better things while at the same time being content with the way things are. Here, we have nothing to lose.

The story above describes the strength of our inner being, our true, innermost core, and the importance of being able to recognise it. It describes the importance of unleashing its power and how it helps us to achieve the right focus. Here, we feel that we have everything. Here, the focus is on the right thing. The focus is on what we already have and are, not on what we don't have and believe we must have, or on what we are not and believe we must be. This is how some people are able to think they have everything when this isn't actually true, while others don't realise they have everything even though they do.

I can't tell in advance whether my opponent in Ankara has everything or nothing. And that's not what's important. What's important is how she *perceives* her situation, her life, what she has and doesn't have, what she is and isn't. In the final, in that moment of performance, two athletes – and two perceptions – face each other. The one who believes she has the least to lose has the greatest advantage.

This is an insight that will turn out to have remarkable value, not only when it comes to achieving our goals but also in terms of being satisfied here and now.

But first, we should accept that it's asking too much to expect us to constantly be aware of and see our life in a favourable light compared to the lives of so many others. This requires us to carry out a continuous external analysis of other people's situations that are far from our own, to compare this with our own situation and also to have the energy not to let niggling worries get the upper hand. Since the world around is usually – quite naturally – limited to our own little bubble, this isn't easy. And it's only when we ourselves are completely satisfied that we can look up and focus on something other than our own minor ailments, our failings and the greener grass on the other side of the fence. How then can we be completely satisfied and look up?

Well, first and foremost it would be impossible to satisfy all our desires and needs. This would take every waking hour and would be a lifelong limitation. There's no point striving for an impossibly perfect existence and allowing this to be essential to our satisfaction. In this way, our life and our existence would never be complete.

But what we can do is to grasp the power of our inner being, of our inner core. Focusing on this is a state of *being* that no-one can ever take away from you. It is satisfaction in itself. It requires nothing other than what *is*. In order to recognise this inner core, you must detach yourself from both what you have achieved and what you want to achieve. If you detach yourself from this for a moment, you automatically identify with your inner core, your true identify and your inner value. Compare this with the focus model – focusing on what exists requires you to put aside thoughts about the past and the future for a while.

Take the match against my Chinese opponent as an example. Imagine it's *you* at the shooting range in Fort Benning. It's *you* who have trained your way into the ranks of the world elite, and are looking to win against this person who, in purely technical terms, is slightly better than you. You are the underdog. You notice that you have identified strongly with the image that you will win. Now the equation has changed – the opposition you face is better than you, but you must win at any cost. Nor can you draw on all the training you have done over the years, for no matter how you think about everything you have invested and all the hours you have put in, the opposition has trained more. You don't have the chance to become more skilled than you have become up until this moment. You are no longer convinced that you will win, and this scares you. How will you solve this? Who are you if you don't win? That is the question. It is also the core of this way of thinking.

Now detach yourself from everything you have achieved so far and your need to win, simply embrace what *is*, and you will soon feel some small sign of power. What you can feel is the power of your inner core. Your actual intrinsic worth. You are the same, whether you win or lose. We all have access to this power, whoever we are and wherever we live. No well-being, no hours of training, titles, medals or skills can better strengthen our ability. Here, you are identified with your inner being and your focus is right. This is how the strength in our inner being can defeat a superior opponent.

And those of us who live where we already have everything should be aware that it is easier for us to reach this state than it is for those who strive for a better life in the name of survival. And yet it was this power in his inner being that Alexandr also found, despite his spartan lifestyle and his ambitious goals. He succeeds in disregarding everything that *is to come* if he wins, and everything that *will not come* if he loses, and faces his opponent with a powerful *being*. This is the way to achieve a focused mind. It was this that shone through in his unconcerned, clear-sighted attitude, and is what in all probability made him an Olympic champion a few years later.

As we have seen, we tend to end up following a pattern whereby the worse things go, the harder we train or work. Many of us try to compensate for a lack of skill, experience and intelligence by at least being diligent. Our self-esteem and our intrinsic worth are found in quantitative training and in everything we do as opposed to what we actually are.

This has a negative impact on our inner core, which risks losing more and more of its power in the face of all the external pressures to achieve skill and perfection.

The fact that we work in this way and react strongly if we lose, don't get or don't succeed with what we have imagined is because we have strongly identified ourselves with our history and our imagined future. Our outer being thrives on thoughts of ourselves, of our past and future successes. The more we identify ourselves with the skill, the medals and the awards we have achieved or see ourselves achieving, the more it thrives. Our outer being depends on us achieving or believing that we will achieve, and is powerless in the *now*. Our inner core, on the other hand, is not dependent on anything more than the now. Presence.

Imagine a core surrounded by your outer being, all the thought structures that are kept alive by identifying with what you have been and will be. Like an orange, or even better like a sun – that can keep on growing without limits, but with an outer being that draws its energy from the core. Even if the core is only two percent of the sun's entire volume, it accounts for half its mass. This tiny core is your actual identity, your very own value. It is a greater asset than the sum of everything you can achieve outwardly.

It is here that we find the person behind the symbols of rank, the conquests and the medals.

Here is the power in *I am*, which is intentionally written in the present tense because no real being can exist in the past or the future. Experiencing this power is an incredibly liberating and immense feeling. *I am* is a more powerful tool than *I am it* and *I am this, I have been this* or *I will be this*. It is being fully present. Focus is nowhere other than in *the now*, and here lie your unlimited capabilities.

When we instead identify with our outer being, with more knowledge, more titles and even more skills, instead of replenishing and identifying with our inner core, there is a risk that the core will shrink. Some goal-focused people may even find that their inner core shrinks to almost nothing. Thoughts of the future and pursuing new skills will then have all the power. Almost all self-worth is dependent on the outer being. Here, the focus is only on what will be.

If a goal-focused person doesn't succeed in her goal and cannot draw upon her inner core, her thoughts will turn back to the past, creating an identity at breakneck speed that relates to the unachieved goal: I have a doctoral degree. I am a Colonel. I have trained for 30 hours a week. I am world champion.

Note that everything which fills our outer being, what we have done and will do, is also what we get a response to. It is what we deliver in our work, our training reports, our titles and our medals. Things that others see. These are what we get external praise for. A strong inner core cannot be seen outwardly in the same way. Its power is not measurable. Its ability is instead seen in the form of contentment and calm. It is only outwardly visible in that apparently impossible tasks are completed, a great calm is maintained in chaotic situations, and desire prevails in the face of opposition.

It is important not to misinterpret our outer being and our inner being as if our inner core would cope without the outer being. It's not wrong to be proud at what you have fought for, endured, won or achieved. Quite the opposite! It would be a shame to strip life of these pleasures. The main thing – and the only important thing – is not to identify only with this, but also and ideally mostly to identify with your inner core.

One question relating to performance that you can ask yourself from time to time to make it easier to keep focusing on your inner core is whether it is you yourself who wants to win at any cost, or whether it is your outer being that won't allow you to lose at any cost.

As a shooter, I realised a while after my career, and particularly after having got to know successful former athletes from completely different sports, such as ice hockey, that the fact shooting is both little known and unglamorous is a mental asset. Since success never resulted in fame, big sponsorship deals or professional contracts, I could be certain that my efforts and my drive were always based on passion, and not on my external need for recognition, praise or more money. How else would I have stood alone in those damp basement ranges, year after year? I didn't have much to draw on other than my inner core.

In this way, those who compete in sports that attract media attention and more money face a different challenge, particularly after their careers. They must constantly take care to ensure that their focus remains on their passion for the sport, and does not drift over to external desires for continued fame. For these people, identifying with external praise, attention and response is all too easy. Losing or reaching the end of their career can then create a deep emptiness compared with a situation where the focus is on the inner being and nothing that is actually vital can be lost.

Our inner core is not afraid to lose. Not in the least. It has nothing to lose, because it does not identify either with what has been done or what will happen in the future. It just is.

Because we are so willing to go where we get a response and work hard to feed our outer being, we easily stray from identifying with our inner being.

Everyone's inner core should therefore receive more praise and recognition, more often, from those around us – both at home and at work. It may be immeasurable and elusive, but it is certainly what – despite its lack of visibility – often lies behind great and unexpected success. Praising the way someone *is*, rather than what they *do* or *have done* would be beneficial.

The point here is that it's all about finding a healthy balance between focusing on the external and focusing on the internal. Identify and focus on the inner core in order to be able to make use of its power in stressful situations, when you find yourself at a disadvantage or when you feel insecure. Let your inner core be your source of power. Our outer being, our skill and our successes are changeable and thus less reliable. The inner core is always within reach. It is unchangeable and is always replenished by focus. The stronger the core, the greater the chance of success.

When I encountered the Chinese shooter, I first looked desperately for something in my outer being with which I could conquer my opponent. Stressed, I searched for something that could make me better and more skilled than I actually was at the crucial moment. An impossibility. My outer being was ultimately empty of reserves, and the realisation that I was the underdog – unable to improve anything – was terrifying. However, this insight was a healthy and concrete moment of self-examination – the cold, hard facts that I needed in order not to completely lose my grip of the situation. Shifting from nervously searching for resources in my outer being, and shifting into *being* and finding access there to my inner core and my actual self-worth was, in its very simplicity, incredibly clever. Here, I lacked nothing. I had nothing to lose.

Now think of my Chinese opponent as a symbol for any competitor. Having been superior in terms of her skill and her background training, she suddenly encountered someone who had nothing to lose. Facing someone who isn't afraid to lose is the most terrifying opposition of all.

Our inner core copes with adversity well – all the blows and all the times when the circumstances aren't as we wanted or expected them to be. The nicest comment I recall having heard in this context was from my neighbour, a wise old lady with a cat, when we met in the park outside the apartment complex where I was living at the time. She had recently read a report in the local paper saying that I had missed out on the Olympics once again, and she knew that sport meant a great deal to me. As I petted her cat, she said:

"You're not going to the Olympics?"

"No, I'm not," I replied quietly without looking up from the cat. The lady fell silent for a while. Then she said:

"Oh, well. You'll have to do something else then, and I'm sure it will turn out well."

What a simple yet insightful comment! There I was, sulking at not achieving one of my goals, when she reminded me that I have a value outside that goal. That, in her eyes, I have the capacity for something else – that I should simply move on. She commented on my inner value, not my outer value.

The worst thing many of us can imagine is being left by a partner and maybe having to give up everything we've built up together. Who are we, then? Perhaps we have to move from our dream house into somewhere small, lonely and cramped. Or maybe the opposite – daring to leave all this behind … How would we manage? Losing a job and becoming unemployed is also a challenge. Psychology shows that different people cope differently with such a setback, and that this depends largely on how strongly they identify themselves with their job.

Some people quickly adopt a new way of thinking, see new opportunities and remain proud, while others see their entire identity come crashing down. Perhaps some people naturally identify themselves more easily with their inner being, making them bolder in their approach. These individuals appear to cruise through life with greater ease than those whose minds are anchored in what they *do* and not in who they *are*. But no-one escapes unscathed from a separation or an unexpected redundancy. Absolutely no-one. But everyone has access to their inner core. This is a state everyone can reach. We therefore sometimes see those who appear to be the weakest overcoming the harshest of setbacks remarkably well. We see the most fascinating and unexpected successes being performed or achieved by the people we least expected to succeed in this way. This is when they have defeated a superior opponent with a power from a dimension that we cannot imagine – a limitless *small core* in our inner being. So is there no desire or need in this core? Is the core always satisfied and contented? If so, one may well wonder what one is doing in the final of a World Championship … Exposing oneself to such pressure would then be entirely meaningless.

Yes, the core is always satisfied and free from desire. But it doesn't lack drive. Research shows that drive comes from within. Your genuine desire to perform and achieve great things is still there, and it's when you take your core as your starting point that your ability to perform is in its element. That's where focus lies. No energy is wasted on thoughts that are unrelated to performance, and you have nothing to lose thanks to the fact that your thoughts are not identified with any ownership at all. You simply are, and you need nothing more than what you are right now. This can be compared to a meditative stage, but fully conscious and extremely sharp. Now you are extremely powerful.

Think for a moment about what could be possible in a situation of such being, where there is nothing to lose.

One medal more or less makes no difference now. Win or lose – the core remains just as stable. That's what makes it so powerful. Only here can someone imagine they have everything. Only here can the gratitude that our lives so deserve become robust. Now it is possible to move beyond the desire for self-actualisation. Only now can we focus on new dimensions, dimensions that are greater than ourselves.

It is now that we can calmly and without shame acknowledge our failings and our as yet unachieved wishes, and say – as Alexandr did – "Shooting not so good", while still honestly declaring that "Life is good!" Only now is the mind ready to focus on what benefits others. In symbolic terms, the World Championship medal is now only a step along the way towards a different, higher goal.

With this mental attitude, people want and dare to set their sights higher than their own desires, whatever their status in life, and whatever their titles, medals or lack of salary bonus. And so Nelson Mandela dedicated his life to defending human value without calculating his own personal cost. In all likelihood and in all hope, it is from this position that decisions of global importance are made by great leaders and those in power. Achieving focus from such a small core in such significant situations is an exceedingly admirable art that is worth striving for.

And now I turn my focus from great leaders to you. From your inner core, you can find your own dimension that is higher than your self-actualisation. As a bonus, this also leads to your self-actualisation goal becoming less difficult to achieve, since it is then only part of a bigger context. This is how Alexandr felt in his keen quest for Olympic gold, which in turn brought new opportunities for his entire family. This is how I felt as I strove towards the World Championship title, which in turn makes it easier to reach out with my message.

In simple terms, the argument is about where the focus should be. If our focus and identification are in our outer being, our minds risk being locked onto goals that don't go beyond the need and the desire for a response. In this way, we will never be entirely satisfied. If, instead, our focus is on our core, we are free to set our visions as far away from ourselves as we want. Our inner being is satisfied from the outset, and absolute freedom prevails in our mind. Achievements that are greater than ourselves are entirely possible. Since the focus is not on satisfying our immediate desires of getting a quick response, this also paves the way for a long-term approach and for making more decisions that are well thought-out. Perseverance is no longer a battle. This also benefits our ability to keep our focus on a single thing for longer. We pay more attention to long-term worldly goals, and we also dare to focus on things that will not pay dividends until long after our own lifetimes.

A pure desire to ultimately do good for others is what dominates. A focus that drives the world in the right direction.

The point is to identify with the core within, a being that I have chosen to call the inner core. Detaching ourselves from external and usually fairly banal everyday desires, and thereby shifting the focus, is valuable not only for ourselves, but also obviously for those closest to us.

EMPATHY – A WAY TO ACHIEVE FOCUS

A particularly special memory of mine is a two-week winter training course during my first year of officer training. We set off from a small village at the foot of Kebnekaise, a mountain in the far north of Sweden. We walked and walked and walked, and the temperature dropped and dropped.

The cold was our worst enemy, and we needed to be more vigilant than normal. Battling against the wind, we walked in single file, stopping frequently to turn and look at the face of the person behind us, particularly the nose, to check for signs of frostbite.

I specifically remember one night when we had pitched camp and were lying close to each other. As was often the case, I was the only girl, but I was far from being the shortest. I normally like to curl up into a little ball, especially in cooler temperatures, but here we lay, squeezed together, like stiff matchsticks in a circle around the fire. When I was woken to take my turn at keeping watch, my feet were red hot from being so close to the fire, while large clumps of ice had formed in my hair by the canvas of the tent.

I now had to crawl up, get dressed, gather my equipment and make my way past and over the other slumbering matchsticks for my watch.

I carefully and silently picked my way over my companions' legs and feet. I had made a sport of never waking anyone at these times.

And so I finally reached my post and sat guard over the fire and my sleeping friends, a tired and motley group of lads. Some snored more than others, and each had his own peculiarities and his own talents. During the daytime, out in the cold, I was dependent on them. In all honesty, I could only dream of achieving their physical strength. But now, here in the night, they were under my protection.

Tired and exhausted in the middle of the night, I reflected on how easy it was to stay focused. The thought of my friends' wellbeing, the feeling of their sleepy but comforting presence, and the joy of watching them rest after a day of tough hiking and digging, was the best trigger for wakefulness and focus. I kept my focus up, motivated and untroubled.

Perhaps that was the first time I reflected on the fact that empathy and focus go together, but on closer consideration this link can frequently be seen.

In theory, empathy is primarily divided up into affective and cognitive empathy. Affective empathy is feeling what another person feels – what often makes us say "I felt that" when we see someone injure themselves, and what we experience as parents when we immediately direct all our focus onto our little baby when it starts crying or screaming. It's what makes us automatically yawn when someone else yawns, or laugh when someone else laughs. Saying that the other person's feelings are "reflected in ourselves" is a good expression, as it involves mirror neurons in the brain which reflect feelings. This form of empathy is unconscious and is rooted in the part of the brain that controls emotions. It is initiated from here, and is directly linked to our survival. At the age of just six months, we can see how a crying baby starts other nearby babies crying inconsolably, for example at a post-natal group, whereupon all the mothers direct their focus on soothing and calming their babies, and no-one is paying the slightest attention to the midwife's explanation of breastfeeding, moving on to solids, colic and so on.

We can also recognise what state someone else is in: frustrated, angry, afraid, sad, dejected or happy, elated, proud or engaged. This happens on a more cognitive level.

Cognitive empathy involves understanding other people's feelings and being able to see things from their perspective. We can put ourselves in their shoes, thoughts and feelings, and basically understand what is being felt in the other person and in oneself. This is a capacity for insight which usually means that we also feel sympathy and want to help and support the person who we understand is sad or in pain. We are conscious of this empathy in a different way to affective empathy. Feeling grief and pain with someone else, for example, but knowing on a conscious level that this is not one's own pain is an indication of cognitive empathy.

Research, headed up by German neuroscience researcher Tania Singer, deals with a refined level of empathy that she prefers to call compassion. This is characterised by the way it does not cause pain. It is not sympathy but concern that we feel, and this is not disturbing in the same way. It is a feeling of warmth and consideration. Professor Singer's research has shown that a feeling of compassion engages different parts of the brain to those that indicate pain. Instead, it engages the parts of the brain that relate to positive reward and are therefore highly constructive rather than disturbing. And this is what I felt for my friends in the cold of the night.

To explain the form of empathy that is instead disturbing, I would like to take another example that led me to realise that focus and empathy go together:

As I mentioned before, my mother helped me untiringly during various forms of training. Her egg sandwiches kept me going through my relentless training in Morup. This was on my home turf, but my mother also accompanied me to competitions around Sweden from time to time, particularly during the period when a place on the national team could not be taken for granted. If I hadn't succeeded in scraping together sufficiently high scores during a particular period at local competitions, I spent my weekends travelling to as many qualifying competitions as possible ahead of a particular date. The level of competition at these events was unimportant. The main thing was that they were listed on the association's website, so the scores counted as qualifying scores. A typical weekend might start on the Friday with a late afternoon match at the former military base in Kviberg near Gothenburg. I might then head southeast to Anderstorp near Gislaved in Småland, where the day would begin with a freezing cold morning match at a small shooting range in the forest. After this, my quest for qualifying scores might take me to Fagersta in Västmanland County to shoot in a "double test" – two matches on the same day – on the Sunday. I could then return home with four matches under my belt.

My mother usually accompanied me on one-day shooting trips. She was the best possible company, she could help carry equipment, and of course she provided the egg sandwiches. It is admirable that, despite having no particular interest in shooting, she would follow me around the country and sit for hour after hour on wooden benches, watching dedicated shooters do their thing. However, we always had a great deal of fun which, of course, improved my chances of success. Once when she was with me at a small forest shooting range at Ringamåla in Småland, with the prospect of a four-hour outdoor match, something happened.

It was clear, cold day in early spring, with just a few hardy shooters at the range. There were no digital monitors here to show the results. The targets moved on a rail that was started at the push of a button. I used the binoculars that I had rigged up on a camera stand to see where each shot had gone without having to drag the target back and forth every time. I also used the binoculars to check on the light conditions, wind and mirage (a natural phenomenon that creates an optical illusion on damp days whereby the air shimmers, so that distant objects appear to move). This is hard to see with the naked eye, and my poor mother could hardly see anything – neither where my shots were ending up nor the conditions I was contending with. Still, we had agreed that she would sit there behind me. The plan was that her presence would sharpen my focus.

Everything was going according to plan at the beginning of the match, but then it started to rain. The damp made its way into the range and under our clothes. I had a cap and scarf ready, but what about my mother? My own mother. My poor mother on a cold bench. No matter how hard I tried to focus, I couldn't help thinking that my mother was freezing. My mother is the most wonderful person in the world. Every time I succeed in something, I know deep down that she is part of it. Sometimes, everything she gave me and my brother when we were young feels so big that nothing I ever do can compare with the efforts she must have made in being our mother. I will always be in her debt. How easy is it to focus on a target 50 metres away with your mother shivering on a wooden bench? I was ashamed to be standing there, and tried to win at any cost. It felt stupid. Deep inside, I grew stressed and wanted time to rush along so that we could drink hot chocolate and go home. I tried to be strong and focused, and to ignore the cold. I tried to be as cool as the day, to focus and dominate like the ice-cold master I can be. But I couldn't. I didn't want to.

Thoughts of my mother quickly took up much of my focus. I fired off a few shots as if I had eyes in the back of my head. A shot, and even before it had reached the target my thoughts were heading in the opposite direction to my mother on the wooden bench, from one of my interests to the other. She must be sitting there on the frozen wooden bench, risking getting cold right thorough. All this, just so I could stand here and do my thing – what nonsense! Or had she gone? Was she sitting in the car? Were there any more blankets or jumpers or anything in the car? I took a break to turn round and have a look. My mother was happy, contented and uncomplaining but, in all honesty, she was freezing. I reluctantly returned to the match without having resolved the problem, and I didn't secure any qualifying scores to speak of on this occasion.

Despite the importance of qualifying scores, empathy (cognitive empathy) took over. My thoughts about how my mother was doing kept on returning, and had the opposite effect to what we both would have wanted. Empathy and focus went together. But not in the most favourable way. My empathy for my mother left me totally unfocused on what I was actually doing. With this note in my training book, my thoughts naturally turned to the fact that the reverse must be possible. If empathy can leave me *out* of focus, perhaps it can also put me *in* focus. That's actually what happened that night on the mountain. But can we influence this ourselves?

Can we guide ourselves into this beneficial empathy, into compassion that focuses us?

There is a part of the brain called the *temporal parietal junction*, or the TPJ. Here, the ability to screen off the mind from emotional influence and stay focused in even the most emotionally chaotic situations can be developed. Doctors dealing with crises, such as in disaster areas and war-torn regions, often demonstrate the unusual ability to carry out their work despite being exposed to dramatic emotions. However, this ability does not appear to be innate – it has to be acquired through experience.

Although my match in Ringamåla seems trivial in comparison with a doctor's efforts out in the world, the question is whether I could have trained my TPJ and coolly fired off perfect 10s regardless of my feelings for my mother.

Well yes, this probably would have been possible – technically speaking. However, studies have shown that people who are often exposed to emotionally demanding situations such as doctors risk developing a more or less constant blocking of empathy. Their real challenge is often therefore instead to maintain their focus on the task at hand, and *at the same time* to remain open to the patient's feelings and thoughts.

Instead of training my TPJ, I resolved to take my mother only to those matches that were guaranteed to be pleasant and tolerably exciting to watch, in slightly more sophisticated surroundings than cold, draughty ranges with composting toilets. It was clearly easier and healthier to release myself from the idea that my mother's presence would improve my focus than to try blocking the power of empathy for someone I love and care about so much.

And so my problem was temporarily solved. However, this solution did not help me to use the power of empathy in order to sharpen my mind.

Let us return to the focus model and the power of presence and our inner core. What happens in the moment when we experience empathy, or compassion, for those who prefer to use that term? Well, one thing that undeniably happens is that there is no room in this state of mind for other feelings. Obviously, nor is there room for very many egoistical thoughts. Note how hard it is to think in ego terms while also having empathy for someone else. Empathy and compassion thus create a direct route to our inner core and to presence, and hence also to focus. It is hard for empathy to exist in the face of thoughts about the past and the future. Empathy only arises in the here and now. A presence is required in order to be able to feel what someone else feels, and to be able to understand and reflect on this feeling. There's not room for much more in a focused mind.

Being irritated at someone, for example, while also feeling empathy for them is impossible. Nor does empathy stand a chance in meetings with other people if you are still angry about something that has recently happened or that happened earlier in the day. Focusing on what will happen, what the next meeting will bring or what you need to buy for dinner after work has the same effect on empathy for the person you are speaking with. And it's the same when you automatically answer your phone when it rings during a meeting with someone or read a message – in that split second, your empathy, compassion and focus are blown away and it takes time for them to return.

Within this argument there is a distinction that is worth drawing. This is the distinction between carrying out a task all by yourself, such as at the shooting range in Ringamåla, and carrying out a task together with others. If we ourselves are working or performing, empathy shifts our focus *from* what we are doing. Then, it is thoughts of and about someone else that make us feel what we feel. Our thoughts are not on what we are doing. It is therefore most sensible at the shooting range and in similar situations to first overcome the cause of the empathy, since it does not actually add any value to the task. To put it simply, do something about it.

A doctor in a stressful situation cannot change the patient's condition. We, on the other hand, who are performing as I did at the shooting range in Ringamåla, can change our surrounding circumstances in most cases.

If you're sat at your desk wondering how your colleague further down the corridor is feeling after having lost their job, and particularly if things have gone so far that you've started to avoid them because you don't know what on earth to say, then go up to them and be present – your inner core will take care of the rest. This action is far better than just sitting there unfocused, staring at your computer.

Whatever the situation, it's a matter of providing an outlet for empathy, for compassion. It probably won't take much time, and trying to avoid it will consume more of your energy than surrendering to it, even if it might feel troubling in some cases. The few minutes it might take can easily be made up in the next task thanks to the sharper focus that comes as a result.

In our co-existence with other people, empathy and compassion are always positive, shifting us into focus. A focus on the here and now, on the interpersonal meeting. It is in our meetings with other people that the power of empathy has its greatest value, when it comes to focus.

If you can find that feeling of empathy and compassion in a meeting with someone, the door to focus has been opened and the meeting takes on a completely different nature. Shifting the focus from yourself to the person you are speaking with might sound simple, but it isn't always easy. It requires self-awareness, self-examination and focus.

Imagine a work meeting that is important to you, maybe a sales meeting, a job interview, a pay review or an interview with someone you really respect. How do we find empathy in such a context?

First and foremost, as in all the previous contexts, it is about being aware of what you are thinking and feeling. In a conversation, *noticing* an inner irritation, for example, is the first step towards sharper attention. As soon as you acknowledge it and so accept the situation, you can be rid of it much more easily, and you can begin to open up to the other person.

The next key element of this is to trust that your brain will not forget what you want to say in a state of empathy. Despite the focus being placed on the other person, instead of your own needs and thoughts, the brain is perfectly capable of holding onto those threads that you are so afraid of forgetting. This is something that our subconscious is extraordinarily good at. It can remember at least as well as our conscious mind. What is more, it can make many more associations and come up with many more new and original ideas than the conscious mind, which is so afraid of forgetting something. It takes all those things you were afraid of forgetting and delivers them to your consciousness right when you need them most, often in a new and even better form. Empathy is a state of mind that helps the brain to remember rather than to forget. This is because empathy helps allow the subconscious to bubble up and be brought into play. It helps us to achieve a state of relaxed focus, which in turn helps us to say the right thing at the right time, and to pick up on the signals that suggest something should be left unsaid. Empathy helps the brain to know when it is better to listen than to bombard the other person with words that won't achieve the desired effect. It allows scope for the brain's intuition to kick in and for the meeting to head off in a wholly unexpected direction. Exciting diversions can occur that are more rewarding than you initially thought possible.

Before we can reach a genuine state of empathy, we thus have to let go of thoughts regarding our self – our own wishes and needs - and foremost the anxiety that, in our empathy for the other person, we will forget what we actually wanted to say. This means having focus. Not on ourselves and our own thoughts, but on the other person's. A kind of mutual understanding. A warm and pleasant feeling. A presence.

Research has shown that training in reading other people's facial expressions increases a person's capacity for empathy. And in every context where we are opposite another person, we can practise letting go of thoughts of ourselves and focusing on the other person's face. Focusing on small details, small nuances, real and fake smiles and subtle movements in the corner of the eye will give your empathy more and more of a hold over your brain. Eye contact is enough, since our peripheral vision captures the rest, and our eyes actually reveal a great deal. The genius thing about this focus on facial expressions is that it helps us to understand what is being said without words, and that can be an awful lot.

Empathy can, of course, also arise simply by intellectually reasoning your way into that state. Imagine you are a manager and you want to be better at focusing your mind and being more present in every meeting. Here is a simple tip: every time you are about to meet someone "under" you, think back to how you felt when, earlier in your career, you had done all your preparations and were nervously waiting for a meeting with one of your superiors. This memory will help you to put other thoughts to one side. The past, the future and you yourself are unimportant in that moment, and the focus then falls on your empathy for the person nervously entering the office.

Research has shown that power, status and rank can have an impact on the capacity for empathy. A person in a subordinate position is better at reading another person's facial expressions and emotions than one with a high rank, a lot of power or a high social status. It seems that we find it easier to spontaneously focus on those who could mean something to us in terms of status, which probably has evolutionary roots.

This is worth bearing in mind, particularly for those in our society who work at a high level and are so well placed that they don't actually need to rely on other people's engagement with them.

We have discussed the value of presence in meetings and we have also noted how difficult it is, in meetings with other people, to be irritated and at the same time feel genuine empathy. As mentioned before, many people, usually those with a busy diary, feel impatient and frustrated in meetings when things take too long. In actual fact, this depends largely on where the focus lies – on themselves and their needs and wishes, or on the person sitting opposite them. If the starting point is one's own interests, knowledge and capabilities, rather than those of the other person, it is not surprising that the otherwise fruitful understanding between two individuals fails to materialise. A mutual understanding has a surprisingly productive value whatever the nature of the meeting, be it a performance review, pay review, interview, sales meeting, negotiation, brainstorming or coffee break. Such an understanding builds trust. Even if the purpose of the encounter is to gain an advantage or secure a deal, it is always useful to understand the other person's inner feelings and to be able to read what is being communicated non-verbally. The way to read hidden messages in another person involves having empathy for the person in question, however difficult, dull or irritating you might find them.

Remember my attempt to perform on the shooting range with my frozen mother on the wooden bench? Just as empathy for someone we really care about can make us *lose* our focus, in meetings with someone we don't know as well or don't even like, when empathy doesn't feel quite natural, we can *choose* to feel empathy and in so doing *find* our focus.

Empathy requires paying attention to the small details in another person. It requires a state where your thoughts are not darting off in every other direction. That means being present, and once again presence is what one needs if the goal is a focused meeting.

You might now be thinking "no matter how present, empathetic and focused I am, things still don't go the way I want every time." Of course, you would be quite right.

And it is as true for me as it is for anyone.

It All Fell Apart

It's a World Cup competition in a witheringly hot Bangkok and the match has just begun. We're shooting in the prone position. It's going very well. I've hit three inner tens in almost exactly the same spot. I take a quick pause for a slug of water, without changing my position. I take the little towel and wipe the perspiration from my face. Putting the towel back, my hand hits the water bottle and I make a quick attempt to stop it falling over. I lose my balance and my rifle sways off line. In my tight position, my arm goes with it and my elbow is twisted against the hard floor. The pain is excruciating. I lose control and roll around on my back.

Officials hurry to my aid. They think the blonde shooter has heatstroke. I have to stop my match. The language barrier means that no-one understands it's just my elbow that's the problem. I'm taken away in a wheelchair, surrounded by concerned locals. This swarm of people, with me at its centre, fills the corridor behind the competition lanes and shooters warming up for the next round are forced to clear a path. At the end of the corridor we rush past Roger, who is doing some stretching. Our eyes meet briefly but I have no time to explain either in words or gestures.

Roger found it tough to complete his match amidst the distracting bouts of empathy and concern about what had happened to his shooting mate and gave an unremarkable performance. I spent the rest of my time in Bangkok with an injured elbow, and we both left Thailand without an automatic place in the Olympic team. I later made an appearance in the local newspaper, looking like a dejected baby owl, under the headline: "Burst bursa sac keeps Christina from Olympics". In truth it should have said "lack of care" rather than "burst bursa sac". The headline made the incident sound like terrible bad luck, as if there was no doubt I would have made it into the Olympic team if only I hadn't injured my elbow. That wasn't the case at all. Securing an Olympic place is never a dead cert with such small margins at play. In that match I also still had 57 shots to get right, and who can say whether they would all have hit the mark if the elbow injury hadn't happened?

In time, the memory of this moment shone a comical light on all the hard work. Here we were, Roger and I, having trained like crazy for weeks. Dressed in all our shooting kit, we had stood on balancing blocks in the sauna for hours on end, rifle in hand, practising how the body reacts in the heat. We had got ourselves into good shape and, happy and motivated, we had flown to the other side of the world to try for success once again, with the same conviction we always had. And when the day came and it felt like nothing could go wrong, Roger watched me being wheeled out of the arena in tears. Could this have been any more of an anticlimax?

At the time, I was so upset and angry that on the journey home I was tempted to put the wrong address label on my rifle case and the case containing all my shooting kit – just let it all be carried off to who knew where.

But now, a few years later, I still giggle at the thought of the wonderful contrasts and all the ups and downs involved in this struggle for success. After three miserable shots, my time in Bangkok was rendered utterly meaningless. A second's lack of focus and all my chances were blown away on Thailand's searing wind.

Isn't that often the way it goes? We enjoy the fight, but mostly we have our wings clipped and we fall back down to earth, blaming bad luck and unforeseen incidents. Wouldn't we all have been world champions if only one thing or another hadn't happened?

If we think about it, life is very much made up of small margins. It's rarely the big steps that lead to major success. It's more the small changes and incremental improvements over time that slowly but surely take us in the desired direction. And so it is with small margins and minor incidents that snowball into disaster. You never have all the margins on your side. All our lives hang by a kind of marginal thread, sometimes to our benefit and sometimes to our detriment. And these margins are hard to have any control over. They are simply part of life's excitement and unpredictability. Only patience and perseverance can have a fair chance against the unexpected, the coincidences and the little mistakes that play practical jokes on our lives and our work.

One such tiny mistake, which wouldn't even normally be called a mistake, was made by my Michael on the first day that we moved into our house to finally live under the same roof, after years of shuttling about and snatching brief encounters at airports around the world. He touched a metal rail in a three-phase electrical box when he was sorting out a pile of cables behind the TV. I was heavily pregnant and there were removal boxes everywhere, but the house was ours. Nothing could possibly spoil the wave of joy I felt. Various minor acts of a careless nature had preceded this incident, leading the previous owner of the house to disconnect the circuit breaker in favour of outdoor lighting. Michael was hit by the full 25 amps. He shook and contorted in a way I had only seen in films, and it lasted so long that his back broke. A simple fracture of the fourth thoracic vertebra. That evening a series of unlucky margins culminated in the worst accident we could have imagined. The shock and the fear of how bad it might be stayed with me over the following days. I had no bed and a baby bump so I slept on the floor. I didn't want to leave the hospital for a minute in case I missed a chance to talk to the doctors who were flocking around Michael. I was active, precise and inquisitive. Will there be an operation? What will happen then? Will he be coming home? Would I end up all alone with a baby? How would I manage that? Why? Why now? One time when I left the hospital to fetch some things for Michael and a few clothes myself, I was unlucky enough to have a puncture on a roundabout. No way! This can't be happening. Not now! I pulled off onto a little gravel track just outside Ängelholm Airport and called a taxi. And there I stood with my bulging tummy. All alone by a field in Skåne's bitter wind, raging at how bad life can be. I can't be standing here stamping my feet. I need to be with Michael – now! I pulled myself together. Tried not to cry. When the taxi arrived, the drive asked curtly: Giving birth? No, my husband has broken his back, I explained equally firmly. Then I just fell apart. I cried and cried, and my bulging tummy had never felt as poorly timed as it did now. Please, please little one, stay in there as long as you can, I begged. Mummy isn't ready.

But after some time at the hospital and on the very day before I was due to give birth in this chaos and uncertainty, I was suddenly hit by the fact that Michael must have been lucky. For some unknown reason, the current had chosen to earth itself through Michael's back, which he happened to have leaned against the wall, instead of through his body and through his heart.

No-one survives 25 amps through the heart. Mere millimetres from the heart, the current had changed direction and burned its way out through the shoulder. A succession of small margins had caused a macabre accident but left the victim living. Most of the margins had actually been in Michael's favour – considering the circumstances and the emotional depths they took us to, we have nothing to be sad about. This is perfectly captured in a photo taken by one of the doctors: Michael is lying in his hospital bed and I'm standing next to him, with my pregnant stomach looking like a ball in the centre of the picture. Both our smiles are relaxed and we are bursting with emotion. A kind of focus on the rollercoaster of life. I sometimes look at that photo to remind myself of the unpredictable rules in the game of life, and the joy of playing anyway.

Inevitably, with small margins come ups and downs. At the point in my career when I was well on the way to my goal, and I was an established shooter at both national and international level, a serious loss would surprise many of the people around me. Particularly the less experienced shooters, who lived under the illusion that a shooter of Christina Bengtsson's calibre must at least always reach the final. But I wasn't surprised. I had learned that behind every success lies a whole string of losses.

The first time we met, Björn Larsson, a good friend and something of a mentor, asked me how I was able to continue battling towards my goal with such enthusiasm and enjoyment, despite all the losses. I told him straight:

"It was only when I started reconciling myself with not always winning that I began to achieve the really big wins."

It was that simple. And just as the shooting victories began to fall into place thanks to this insight, so did other things in life. It shouldn't be underestimated, however, just how much time this insight takes. You need practice in losing so the brain can learn to deal with this phenomenon.

Precision shooting is therefore immensely educational. The margins are so exceptionally small that it is very uncommon for the same shooter to win two major championships in a row. The competition is so tough that several thousand competitors around the world have a shot at the championship title. Many thousands of shooters equal the world record in training several times a season, sometimes several times a week. A shooter's physique provides no indication of who is in form ahead of a championship, and the person who recently shot top points in a competition could take a wrong turn mentally in the next competition and blow any chance of reaching either the final or the podium. It all depends on what thoughts are thought and why. There is an established world elite that takes it in turns to step up onto the podium, but even they will stand in the audience surprisingly often, applauding the medal winners of the day. A single millimetre can mark the difference between gold and a place in the stands.

All experienced shooters are used to losing. American Matt Emmons is one of the world's best shooters and at Athens in 2004 he was well on the way to securing two Olympic golds. With one gold already under his belt in the prone shooting, Matt was facing his last shot in the standing final, on his way to yet another fantastic victory, when he shot the wrong target and ended up coming last. At the Beijing Olympics in 2008, Matt took silver in the prone and was once again leading ahead of his last shot in the standing final. Having had a great run and with a healthy lead of 3.3

points, he hit a 4.4 with his last shot. Again, he failed to win a medal. He called this *"a freak of nature"*, and said the 4.4 was because he had squeezed the trigger a tiny bit too hard and fired a tiny bit too early. A 6.7 would have been enough for gold, and in our world everything outside a 9.0 is considered useless. But it all comes down to just millimetres at a distance of 50 metres, even if the spectators can't see it. Matt has to live with the infamy of missing out on gold on the final shot at two Olympics in a row, despite the fact that he got a bronze in the standing event at London 2012. In this story, the attention is all on the misses, at least outside the shooting world. And that is only natural. It's what brings the spectators and journalists to the shooting range – how is it going to go for the guy who threw away two Olympic finals in a row on his last shot. The fact that he qualified for three Olympics in a row against stiff US competition, and that he won gold and silver in a different discipline and also holds a bronze, gets ignored in our thirst for sensationalism and scandal.

The argument is not that Matt should stand with a drink in his hand and look happy after his misses in Athens and Beijing. Obviously anyone would be hard-pressed to produce a genuine smile immediately after such an ordeal. But never forget the strength of looking at your abilities, skills and self-worth, and being able to choose happiness even in times of loss and when margins and chance change your planned route forwards. That's what Matt did. He persevered in his drive for more medals. And his miss in Athens led to more than just the loss – also at play were margins of a different kind than the millimetres on the target. Amongst the crowd of athletes, officials and journalists, he actually met his current wife, Czech shooter Katharina, for the first time just after the final, when she came up to him to offer her condolences on what had happened.

So after this championship – was Matt a winner or a loser? Considering that he met Katharina, perhaps only because he shot the wrong target, he was surely a clear winner overall. But in sporting terms? He won one Olympic gold and a miss of the worst kind caused him to lose out on another. At two Olympic Games in a row. There are various ways of looking at this, but the only interesting answer to this question is actually what he himself thinks. At the risk of sounding dull and boring, the only right answer from the perspective of focus is "none of the above". There is no great benefit to be gained from identifying yourself as a winner or loser. That simply puts the focus on what *has* been accomplished, not on what *is*. The word *revenge* is so well established that it is used almost on a daily basis. But battling for four years to reach the next Olympic Games in order to get revenge for a previous miss will usually do more harm than good. It results in life being lived in the past and the future, with no focus at all on the present. Something *went* wrong that *will* be put right in the future. In my experience, the most constructive way to handle a World Championship title is to think that I am world champion just for one day. Similarly, I am only a loser for the day that I miss out on a medal, don't reach the final, shoot the wrong target or come last.

The people around me take a different view, however. Once a world champion, always a world champion. Good shooting friends and my coach still call me "Champ". Of course this is a very nice nickname to have, and it's certainly better than "The Hulk", but it doesn't really fit the picture I want to have as I move on to new goals in the most focused way possible.

It is certainly true that getting my first medal took me through a mental barrier, but this feeling brings no advantage in the next championship. Or if it does, then it is only marginal. Think of it the other way round instead, that if you identify with the image of your "gold match" and now have to do it all over again, you are actually in a worse situation than if you were entering the match from square one. Other people will also have upped their game and new competitors will have appeared on the scene, so performing as well as last time is probably not good enough. A gold at the World Championships is won on that one day, under that day's conditions, against the competitors that made it to that day's final. Success in the next tournament requires the same clean slate as before, rather than identifying with or focusing on past achievements.

Sometimes when I'm standing in front of a group of people, giving a speech, I catch a glimpse of wonder and respect in their eyes. They may be impressed to see a world champion on stage. And this is before I've even said hello. They are pre-programmed to think that the woman on the stage who has won a gold medal is cool. In our society, we are so strongly driven by the belief that a person who has once done something extraordinary always *is* extraordinary, that we fail to see the person behind the achievement.

Everyone wants to know how you did it. Some want to know so they can do the same thing. Some want to establish that it would be impossible for an ordinary mortal, and so they don't need to put in any more effort than they already do.

The words "world champion" have a particularly ring to them that instils respect and fascination. Champions are put up on a pedestal, perhaps because a championship title is not something everyone can achieve. It is as if this kind of success has something impossible about it, and the winners' podium is there to sort the wheat from the chaff, no matter how small the margins are.

Many people can't stop themselves asking what the secret is, what it was that made him, her or you the best. It must be something unique. They have a preconception that if a person has reached the level of a world champion, and has thus become the *best in the world*, they must be extremely gifted, extremely goal-oriented, extremely disciplined and probably extremely self-absorbed. So if I show any semblance of being a normally talented, sometimes lazy, often absent-minded, lively but relaxed and not particularly egocentric person, listeners sometimes have a tendency to be disappointed.

Is this because people want it to take something out of the ordinary, and for it to require a painful exclusion of other things in life to achieve success? So they can be clear that not just anyone can achieve elite status? Because if not, then everyone has a chance of going that far – and that would be too much for the ordinary person to bear, knowing that they would rather lie on the sofa than resolutely strive towards something bigger.

The paradox in this is that as soon as we champions begin to see ourselves as champions in the sense of being *better than others*, the medals begin to come at an increasingly slower rate. We always need to return to the kind of self-examination that tells us we are just as mortal as everyone else, and we are all playing with the same small margins. The cold, hard fact must be that a championship title is a *title* and not something on which to hang your whole identity.

In this context, shooters have an advantage over most other sportspeople. Those of us who have lived for years with these irritatingly small margins have all learned that previous successes can't be relied on. Every shooting champion has come 1st one day, and then 8th, 17th, 27th or 52nd the next. Matt Emmons' career is a prime example, although it should be pointed out that he is still one of the most successful figures in shooting history. And life is also like that. No two days are the same and no success, in whatever area, guarantees more.

Success is often ascribed to talent. Talent may be a technical ability or in my case the capacity to put the right pressure on a trigger at the right moment. It might be a physical ability. It might be a particular intelligence. But the most important talent to mention is actually perseverance. The ability to battle on despite successes being conspicuous by their absence. The ability to deal with losing.

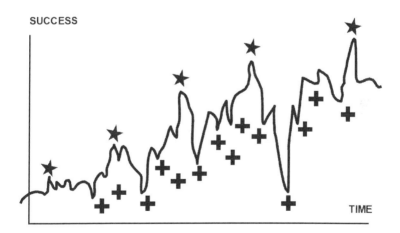

The figure above is a simple representation of the relationship between successes and losses over time. It illustrates the obvious, but rarely mentioned, truth that the times we "stood on the podium" are relatively few and far between, compared with all the times "it all fell apart".

It shows my sporting career from the day I decided to focus on one sport and become the best at it, until the moment I became the best in the world. Job done.

The stars represent successes, but remember that one is only champion for a day. Now note that the timescale we're talking about here is 15 long years. Also note the endless number of matches that have gone badly, marked with a cross in the illustration – all the times I came 48th, 72nd, missed out on the final, came 4th in the Swedish Championships, 4th in the World Championships or became dehydrated, burst a bursa sac or suffered from nerves, only to end the final with a 7 and come last. Finally, look at the stars again and note how few times I was actually top of the podium over all those years. If I were to add up all the minutes I've spent on a winners' podium, it wouldn't even come to a whole day over the course of 15 years. Maybe not even half a day.

And of course, the model applies to all of us who focus on something in life. For corporate leaders, managers in organisations and businesses, sportspeople, artists, researchers and parents, knowing this is the only way to lessen the fear of failure.

If we can learn that, as people with commitment, we live in the field of crosses and learn to be happy there, we won't be as afraid of dropping down there on those occasions when we are supposed to perform at our best. The timeframe of losses is where we live for much of our life, even if we make it into the spotlight now and then. And this is where our focus should lie, in the real world, which is not at all as bad as we might fear. It is when facing the opportunity to achieve a star under the model above – to excel, to win, to shine – that thoughts of *what if…* distract the mind from the task in hand, reducing the chances of success. Practising failure is thus a good exercise to help the mind to focus. If you can learn to handle failure and know that you remain strong at heart, as described in chapter 5, you can enter situations of pressure and performance with a very different energy than you would without this experience. With this knowledge under your belt, there is also no risk in aiming high. Losing is a natural aspect of commitment in all its forms and it is only something to be ashamed of if the loss makes such a major dent in your identity that you are too afraid to try again.

The strategy for practising failure is no more complicated than trying and daring to make mistakes and fail again and again. This takes time. You can't claim the talent of perseverance until you have tried and lost several times over. But it is also a good tactic, as you proceed, to listen to yourself and note how your successes and failures are described in your inner thoughts. If you are really afraid of failing, you should give it more practice. If you can't stop identifying yourself with your earlier successes and titles, you know you should switch focus and instead try to strengthen your *inner core*. That means self-examination to find the cold hard facts that tell you who you are without your previous achievements. Otherwise you will automatically identify just as strongly with a potential future loss and consciously do everything in your power to avoid it. Then your actions will be driven by fear, and your focus will be wrong.

What we tell other people is a clear indication of what is going on internally, where our focus lies. The first time I can honestly say I was able to handle a loss well was when an announcer once came striding up to me carrying a microphone.

Leading the field in the final, I had every chance of winning, but shot so badly that my lead disappeared and I lost out on a medal. I ended up in a miserable 7th place, and now everyone was looking at me wondering how I felt and how it could all have gone so badly. The announcer approached me. He was short, nervous and eager. He was looking for a thrilling and emotional interview on the back of a recent failure. Hot and red-cheeked, I looked him in the eye. "What happened," he asked, pointing the microphone at me. Without any hesitation or evasion, I answered frankly: "It all fell apart." I gave a little laugh, nodded sagely and waited for a follow-up question. The announcer was stunned and fumbled around for something to say, but nothing came. I laughed again, waved to the crowd and left the announcer and the match.

The truth was such as release! There couldn't be a more honest description of a situation that for various – sometimes unfathomable – reasons hadn't gone to plan. That was what had happened, and it doesn't need to be written about in any more complicated terms than that. My comment provided relief because it came from my inner self. There was no focus on trying to appear better than my 7th place, or on feeling that I had to look strong and get to the bottom of this and commit even more, train even harder. It is a statement that also reveals complete acceptance of what happened. The phrasing distinguishes between what went wrong – *it* all fell apart, not *I*. It all fell apart, but it doesn't affect me – so that's that.

Such a comment is not born out of sincerity, but out of a background of long, hard practice in failure.

I never said it in the first three years, when I came last in every competition. I cried inconsolably each time, even during training, when a shot didn't go where I wanted it to and I didn't meet the goal for that day. I sometimes stood long into the night until I'd shot a clean round of 100, ten 10s in a row. As soon as I shot a 9, I forced myself to stop that round and begin again. One night at airbase F7, the victory, i.e. the clean round, didn't come until just after 4:30 am. Madness. But three years of losing was good training, and it was only later that I realised those years were not just about improving technically, physically and in terms of knowledge, but also teaching the brain to accept that things will almost always go a little off target.

It may be impressive that I stuck rigidly to my goal and spent so many nights shooting like a person possessed, in the middle of my physically demanding military service. But looking at the bigger picture, I would probably have done just as well if I had stopped all the madness, written the day off as a bad job and simply gone to bed. The lesson and its value lay in handling the failures, rather than stubbornly never giving in.

As I mentioned before, practising failure takes time, and the beginning of this experience requires particular sensitivity. My niece, who is 14 years old, is a very good singer. We were talking the other day and she told me, entirely unprompted, that before she performed with her singing class at a public concert, she was so nervous she thought she would die. And this was despite her and her schoolmates always singing beautifully.

We often respond to this kind of comment with: "No, you're so good, it'll be fine, there's nothing to be nervous about." But the fact is that her comment "I'll die" is just as sincere as my "it all fell apart". The difference is that she is not yet well practised in either setbacks or misfortune. Nothing but practising the situation itself can change the feeling she has. Practice, practice, practice. Not practice in singing better, but practice in being brave enough to step onto the stage, to be anything but perfect. Practice in the fact that things don't always go well. Practice, practice, practice. Her comment is sincere because the brain has an emotional centre that reacts to external stimuli and judges whether or not what is happening is life-threatening. If the emotional centre decides there is a threat to life, no words can overturn that. Particularly in stressful situations, the emotional centre overrules our intellect. Her choice of the word "die" is thus not all that surprising. In the moment that she goes up onto that stage, she is in principle just as afraid for her life as she would be being chased by a lion on the savannah. Nothing can talk away the feeling that the emotional centre has set in motion, at least not in that moment. Only practice will do that. So what can we say or do to help?

Because her anxiety is genuine, it is better to acknowledge it and say: "How awful!" Who doesn't want other people's understanding of an evidently frightening experience? Under less charged circumstances, you can later encourage her to realise that the only thing to do is to continue singing on stage and be prepared for the same emotion to sweep over her time and time again. Eventually, the emotional centre will learn that even if she sings badly, she won't actually die. And so it will no longer invoke its powers because of a threat to life. Only then can the wise words of the intellect compete with the emotions and get through. Only then can we begin to work on focus. As time passes, the situation will seem less threatening and perhaps even really fun.

For a while, my coach always asked before a match: "What's the worst that could happen?" We both thought this was a good strategy before matches about which I was nervous. This question prompted me, on an intellectual level, to paint a scenario of what could happen if I failed to shoot the points we expected or needed. The worst I could imagine was usually that, as well as coming last in the results table, I shot so badly that I shot the equipment to pieces, including the monitors at the range, and shot ugly holes in the wall. That was as bad as it could get. I certainly wasn't going to lose my life over it. So it wasn't so terrible really. We thought this rational analysis would calm me down. But it never did. There was always something inside me that thought "Oh hell!" and I still quaked in my boots as if a hungry lion had been set loose in the room.

No matter how well I was able to comprehend that the situation couldn't be any worse than placing last in the results table, and in the worst case shooting a few holes in the wall, my emotional centre dominated proceedings, just as it is designed to do. It overruled my common sense, piping up that things weren't at all as harmless as my coach and I said. The key here was to understand the structure of the brain and, above all, to simply go out onto the range and make a fool of myself until my emotional centre realised there were no hungry lions chasing me around the place. Only then could we talk about the power of focus to get me to the top of the podium.

Your thoughts have to take their course, working their way from complete terror to a focus on the *here and now*. And (unless you employ a neutral thought such as *toaster* to remove all distracting thoughts before every occasion, every shot), the way to get there is by patiently practising making mistakes.

The length of time this takes varies depending on the situation and the person. Some situations that we are concerned about failing in occur regularly, while others are rarer. The exercise need not always be performed in the same situation either.

The more different the occasions in which we train the brain to switch from dominant feelings of anxiety to the presence of our common sense, the better able we are to deal with new situations of an uncertain nature.

What happens during the practice itself is that, when you are exposed to precisely what you were worried about, coming last for example, being shouted at by your boss or holding a speech for which you haven't prepared, you learn that it is never as bad as you feared. The brain gets to know that the judgement made by the emotional centre is often exaggerated. Gradually your anxieties decrease even in new and unfamiliar situations, and your intellect takes on a more leading role compared with your emotions.

Of course it is important to choose the right moment for this practice. Some people simply must not make mistakes. A surgeon in an operation. A pilot at several thousand metres. An officer in a tough moment on a mission. A serious error on a tunnelling project could have devastating consequences. In these cases, the anxiety has to be taken seriously and given due acknowledgement – it is there for a reason in all such contexts where lives are genuinely at stake. But if, when faced with such a task, you remain so afraid of making a mistake that the anxiety jeopardises your focus on the work, it should simply be accepted that you're not ready to take on this task.

Here lies the difference between sport and many other professions that we have looked at. In sport, the consequences of a loss, particularly for us here in the West, are never particularly serious from a wider perspective. This hit me with ruthless clarity as my team and I were travelling through Rio de Janeiro's slums in an air-conditioned coach. A police escort cleared the way for us, and we were monitored and protected by security guards both inside and outside the coach as we were transported to the World Games and our accommodation in the Olympic Village, which was built for the 2016 Rio Olympics. The fact that – the wholehearted commitment of myself and all the other athletes, trainers, judges, officials and volunteers notwithstanding – this is *a game* is easily lost in all the sporting excitement. But for those outside the coach, with their little sheds for homes, life is not a game. Their anxieties are absolutely well founded. The injustice hit me hard as, privileged and wide-eyed, I glided past as if I was better than everyone else.

For an athlete in the cosseted world of sport, practising failure is an exercise that risks losing little more than your own pride. In terms of threat to life, giving everything you've got is entirely risk-free.

As a sportsperson, this is worth reflecting on when the nerves creep in ahead of a championship.

But what is success? Is it in the eye of the beholder? Does it depend on what others have done or how good others are? That's what we believe at least…

BEYOND THE COMPETITION

That feeling of being worse than someone else, and even more awfully being worse than *everyone* else, is raw and definitely hits all of us at some time or other. It makes us incredibly sad and angry. We see this in everyone, but above all in those who have a drive to win, but have not yet developed into focused winners who can handle losing. Comparing ourselves with others triggers the prehistoric systems in our brain. It strikes right at the very core of our emotional centre which, as it has always done since time immemorial, battles for survival whatever the situation, competition or job.

This was, of course, particularly important in prehistoric times. Being worst in a group could be disastrous for your life and for the survival of your genes. It was vital not to be the worst in the group to avoid the risk of exclusion.

And in many ways we still behave the same way. Who hasn't felt bad about being excluded from some group or other? Who isn't happy to be considered the best? These remain our leading motivators to this day. They are in our nature, and that is fine. So be it. The difference between then and now is, however, well worth examining.

Nowadays, we have a brain with such a well developed intellect that, if we can find focus and not surrender entirely to our emotions, actually doesn't need to limit us to the narrow parameters that constant comparison entails. These parameters also often place limitations on those around a particular group.

"Best in the world" sounds impressive, but in my case it is actually only "best in the world *at shooting*". There is a higher dimension that goes beyond the comparative dimension, created by evolution, the one we call competition. A dimension that unlocks even greater capabilities and causes even greater sparks of motivation than competition does.

Competition is a positive, usually very enjoyable and essential driver. But if we stick with the goal of *being better than others*, we limit our scope to unlock our inner capabilities. If we can free ourselves from the struggle to "become someone", "become the best", "stand at the top of the podium", we can attain a drive that is not linked to competition and comparison with others. Then we reach a dimension in which our potential is unlimited. Here lies a comparison-free power that is greater than "striving to be the best in relation to others". Here lies the prospect of a genuine drive and belief in our own capabilities. This comparison-free power automatically becomes about doing our best according to the capabilities that are actually within ourselves – not those that we should have or are expected to have. Why be limited by what others can achieve?

Everyone is looking to realise their potential, and the best way to do this is to be forced to do your best. Competition certainly spurs us on to do our best, but if our lives are not at risk it takes more than this to get a person to be the best they can be when it really counts. When required to perform, our utmost capabilities are drawn from our inner potential, which is far removed from the competition. This is where we strive to *be exactly as good as we actually are*. As we have seen, this is encouraged by being in a state of focus as set out in the focus model, and by not battling to be more or better than someone else. Otherwise beating the competition sets the standard, rather than your inner self. This then becomes limiting in various situations and also limits the chance of greater development. The dimension beyond the competition is where we find the truth about what we are truly capable of, and what we are good at *now*. The goal is reasonable and the demands arising from it are thus neither overwhelming nor weak. It is here that our potential for doing our absolute best is at its peak.

Once in Ankara, Turkey, when I expressed all sorts of worries about an upcoming match, my coach put me up against the wall and asked directly: Why is it so important to win?

I remember being astonished by his question. The importance of winning was such an obvious thing and one that I was convinced he was striving for as much as I was. Taken aback and rather disappointed, I replied that I didn't see any point in competing other than to win, which at that time in my career was true. I had no better answer than that. In actual fact, it wasn't my answer that was important here, but the fact that I was forced to think about and question an attitude I had taken for granted since I had first taken up the sport.

A deliciously strong Turkish coffee and a moment of self-examination kicked me into action. In my mind I reworded the answer to the question – the importance of winning was actually part of a drive to avoid losing. Being top of the podium was the only safe place where I was guaranteed freedom from the thought that others are better than me. That is what makes winning so desirable. That is why it is so pleasing to be the best. Winning is a freedom – a freedom from comparisons with others.

The more afraid I am of losing and being worse than others, the more important it is to win – which in fact is simply a desire to avoid second place. Having this as your ultimate driver makes achieving first place that much more difficult.

Once I came to this realisation, I was able to reimagine the importance of winning as a reasonable and pain-free desire to do my best. Just as strong a drive to reach the top, but with a focus on my abilities and not who I am in relation to others.

I gained a similar insight into my thirst for first place in the US Army Marksmanship Unit of Fort Benning, Georgia, where I spent a number of weeks training with the national team of the US Armed Forces. I was the only woman in the group, and I got on well with the impressively well trained shooters there. I loved going to their practice ranges. On the door frame above the entrance stood the sign "Welcome to the home of Champions", a phrase I instantly identified with and that meant I found it very hard to leave the range. I wanted to be in there, in that dim light, with my friends the *champions*, forever. I then carried this sense of belonging, almost cockiness, with me around the world, and home to the trials in Sweden.

Maybe it was tall poppy syndrome, maybe it was jealousy, or maybe it was simply my own anxiety about fitting in that stabbed me in the back on my home turf. I won the trials, but with no sense of jubilation. No-one but me seemed to be pleased with the progress I had made during my time at

Fort Benning. No-one appeared to notice the work I had put in. I found this depressing, and when I was reunited with the Americans, who greeted me with such comparative good cheer, I asked them openly:

"What's the point in winning if no-one notices?" This then also became a topic of discussion outside the shooting range.

And once again, the important thing is not the answer to the question, but the reflections surrounding it. You can't always count on the people around you liking your own progress and success. If it doesn't happen, it is merely clear evidence of the way we humans work. We compare ourselves with others. Very few people have touched the higher dimension that goes beyond the comparative one. A certain amount of isolation is thus to be expected when things go your way.

The crucial thing here is how I view this fact. If the response from others is so important that I lose steam when it doesn't come, my focus is not in the right place. Obviously my focus on what other people think and the importance of being acknowledged for my efforts and my medals is greater than the focus on my passion for what I do.

Successful people stick to what they know and let their capabilities rather than their need for validation steer what they should focus on. They stick to their strategy despite the appearance of competitors. If they focus on one competitor, a new one soon appears from somewhere else.

For the truly successful person, it is not about being the best. It is also not part of a successful person's strategy to try to be the best, and they have no intention of being the best, or any plan to be the best. For them it is a question of *achieving a realisation of what,* in their current circumstances, they *can* become really good at. Everyone wants to be best at something, but few people understand – with self-insight and self-examination and without a need for validation – what they have the potential to excel at. The same is true for all forms of project, engagement and ambition. It is therefore crucial to note when your ambition and attempt to perform is being affected by external comparative forces as, while these may spur you on, they also shift the focus from your own capabilities to others.

Without even thinking about it, we are surrounded by comparative forces wherever we turn, when we are distracted by social media, when we look at a billboard, when we read the celebrity magazines at the hairdresser's, on the street where we live, at the car dealer's and not least at work. We are constantly affected by our surroundings as they demand our attention. It takes more than we might think to determine what we are really good at and where our focus ought to lie. In a time when we are exposed to these future opportunities and demands on a daily basis, we can easily find ourselves being nudged from one thing to another, all the time wanting to be equally good at everything. Our focus is not in our own hands, but is controlled by the automatic attention which, without the presence of the intellect, directs our eyestowards whatever seems important at the time. If we are constantly at the mercy of this automatic attention, our existence becomes splintered and it is hardly surprising that we sometimes become tired. We end up constantly flipping from one genre to the next, attempting to be good, if not the best.

This originates from the way, without any reflection, we compare ourselves with others, want to be like others, follow the norm, the fashion and live up to expectations. Yes we want to be like the others, but preferably slightly better. The influences come from so many directions and so many people that it becomes impossible to live up to all the norms, belong to all the groups and be good at everything we take on. And still, in all this flitting to and fro, we struggle for validation and praise from endless different directions. Out of this comes the good child syndrome from which so many of us suffer. Of course we become very good at an awful lot of things, and we also keep ourselves fit, healthy and attractive, but how often do we focus on what we are absolutely best at, and keep our focus on that? Controlled focus is the kind of focus that stands strong despite external influences and that does not constantly get caught up in external competition. Focus of the consistent kind – on one thing, without comparison to everyone else – is preferable in the vast majority of performance-driven contexts, both short-term and long-term. It usually requires us to consciously choose focus. But sometimes it comes to us entirely unexpectedly, and that is perhaps how most of us gain access to it, and most easily recognise it. Major events in life generally put us in such a state. Moments when we lose a loved one, have an accident that turns our life and that of the people around us upside down, or perhaps fall head over heels in love, are occasions when everything else seems unimportant and our focus automatically falls on the one important issue.

The same thing, in a somewhat different context, happens when a child is born and we soon notice that all our engagement, our attention and focus now goes on the child – an initially testing situation that soon turns into the greatest of joys. It is described in terms of an expanded perspective on life, letting go of any focus on your own needs and putting all your energy into someone else instead. Usually this focus is associated with a twofold free-dom. Freedom from your earlier external demands, but also freedom from comparison and competition with your teammates or colleagues. In the shooting world, this mani-fests itself as follows, ahead of a championship team selec-tion: "Please, take my place – I have more important things to do than fight over a trip to China." This thought may appear tame, and inconsistent with a competitive instinct, but on closer inspection it is absolutely beneficial ahead of a championship, ahead of a performance situation, and in life generally. What it actually says is that your *inner core* is so strong and so valued that nothing can come close to its significance. Neither winning nor losing can tarnish its brilliance. The desire to compete and do your best has not gone away, just the demands and the anxiety about not being worthy if a loss does occur.

The power of your inner core thus hasn't been shaken at all. Quite the reverse. If you embrace this, such incidents in life provide a shortcut to your innermost potential.

This focus during special events in life is, for natural reasons, entirely adequate. Taking care of your child at this time of life is unarguably the very best thing you can do, and compared with so much else it will be the thing you are very best at. What other people think and say, and being the best at masses of different things, will cease to be par-ticularly important. Your focus is trained on one thing and life feels extraordinarily meaningful. Presence is rarely an issue, and nor is the sense of being complete.

Viewed in evolutionary terms, letting your focus fall on your children instead of yourself is not much to shout about. It is not something you really have any control over. Although many trumpet it as a great achievement, as a kind of insight that has finally put them on the right track in life, it is actually just a purely automatic state of focus. All the focus goes on the little bundle in our arms and for a time we are freed from all comparative forces. The things around us play less of a role now, for obvious reasons. It would be remarkable if this *didn't* happen.

Perhaps it is some kind of insight, but how can we carry it with us through the rest of our lives? In sport we have often seen new mothers and fathers perform surprisingly well. It seems a little peculiar, because in this situation none of the old, established rules about the number of training hours or total focus on the goal appear to apply. But it isn't all that strange. In that moment, there is a natural focus on one thing, and anything else, even your own sporting prowess, feels much less crucial. Losing thus no longer holds the same fear as before – which is an incredible advantage. And that's not all – the need to be better than others is also, for the time being, not as strong, and maybe this is what makes the biggest difference.

Why do new parents, for whom all of us in the shooting world at least should have the utmost respect, rarely retain this mental advantage over time? Why do they not continue to perform well for all eternity, if they now have an insight into both their own inner worth and keeping a distance from their goal?

Because it is only when we have control – when we have learned to use our controlled attention and consciously choose where we direct our focus – that we can consider ourselves truly focused. It is then that we can exploit the insight we have gained as new parents. We are conscious that the focus this brings is a natural condition that, unless something is done to preserve it, will soon disappear back to the state that previously prevailed. It is only then that we can choose to retain a distance from what we are fighting for and retain our focus on one thing, rather than jumping wherever our instinctive, automatic attention takes us. It is only then that we can stand strong in our inner core and succeed over time.

Science has not shown any difference between parents and non-parents with regard to their capacity for controlled focus. It may be a shortcut or an advantage, like a door that has opened and stays open for a while, giving a glimpse of a world in lasting, pleasant focus. But everyone can open this door, step through and understand what an existence in focus can mean. It is just that life's different events and meaningful incidents give some of us a hint, a little nudge in the right direction.

When older and a little wiser, many people, whatever their life experience, say they are happy to no longer care quite so much about what others think. These people may be well on the way towards controlled focus. The question is whether they know why, or whether it has just happened.

"Why aren't I doing what I love?" an enterprising man in his fifties, with good financial and intellectual resources, asked me a while ago. I had spent a long time successfully coaching him in everything he was doing, but I had never really seen that genuine passion and joy that we want to see in our devotion to a goal. The question he asked me in all seriousness revealed how a person's potential to focus can be high but it can still be misplaced. He is a high-flier who appears to succeed in everything he does, but with an empty feeling inside.

The answer was obvious. We had simply never thought along these lines, and I can't take the credit for then helping him in the right direction towards more appropriate and focused engagement. It was he who bravely posed a rather key question in the middle of his life. His desire was, as with so many of us, to please, to follow expectations and to excel at everything. A subconscious drive controlled by our automatic focus.

We need to understand how we choose focus if we are to consciously direct it towards what we really want and are best at, and keep it there.

Nowadays, we are exposed to an unreal number of contexts in which to operate, and an unnatural number of arenas in which to shine. But allowing yourself to focus on shining in *all* these, and on competing with everyone else around you, would be to destroy yourself and to fragment and waste your time. In these modern times, it is better instead to take control of your focus.

To find your controlled focus, you must first become aware of your automatic focus. In broader terms, when it is not just about survival and quickly dodging a moose in the road, it is this that flits about and is rooted in our inherited desire to be validated, to be like everyone else, preferably better than others and ideally the very best. It strives for speedy validation, always in relation to others.

The whole phenomenon of striving to be or become the *best* in the sense of "*better than others*" is thus an obsolete philosophy. Such striving is out of step with a life in focus. It shifts the focus from the true power and capabilities we have within us onto what someone else is able to do, how well someone else sings, how many points someone else has, how much someone else earns, what someone else owns, what profit someone else makes or what promotion someone else gets. Of course this can be highly motivating, inspiring, and not least exciting to wrestle with. There is nothing wrong with that, but it is important to note when interest in this becomes so dominant that there is no focus left on what you yourself actually want, and what your actual capabilities are in the here and now.

If my personal best is 597 points out of a possible 600, there is nothing to suggest that, in purely technical or physical terms, I couldn't shoot 600 points. As in many other sports, these last points depend not on well trained physical capacity, or even on tactics that could otherwise be a deciding factor in sports such as cycling, which also operates under extremely small margins. If I can shoot fifty-seven 10s in a row, I can surely shoot three more. But when the world record is 597 points, 598 suddenly becomes very difficult indeed. This is because *no-one* has ever shot more than 597 in competition. The whole difficulty with the sport lies here in the fact that we automatically compare ourselves with others and what others have achieved, instead of focusing on our own capabilities.

On one occasion, I announced a training camp over a weekend titled "Why don't we shoot 600 points?". The aim of these practice days was to pool our resources and establish where the obstacles to achieving maximum points lie.

By Sunday afternoon, a number of points had been flagged up, from choice of ammunition to breathing and holding still. But the only point that really answered the question was: "Always one shot at a time". It sounds so sensible and self evident, but it has a deeper meaning than the obvious one. One shot at a time means that shot 58 is fired without any thoughts about shot 57 and shot 59. Shot 59 is fired without any thoughts about shot 58 and shot 60, and finally shot 60 is fired without any thoughts about shot 59, and without any thoughts that the match is then over and the world record has been beaten.

This means that no thoughts exist about either what we ourselves or anyone else has shot through history. This *is* focus , as represented in the focus model. No thoughts about the past or the future. And also no thoughts about what others have done or are going to do or not do, or what other people think.

For this focus to take effect, we need to remove the restrictive comparison with others. The shots should be fired as if the match was going to continue for all eternity. It is this focus that frees up our capabilities and makes us exactly as good as we truly are. This focus helps us feel gratitude for what is and to stand firm when social media constantly competes for our attention.

You might think that the whole system of competition, all sport and much else besides loses its excitement and its meaning if you take away the comparison with others. The whole of our society is, after all, built on competing forces, in one way or another. But we needn't concern ourselves over whether we can be completely freed from comparison with others. This force is so deeply rooted within us that it would be impossible for the structure of our brains to be without it. The point is to take note of it, and then choose to unshackle yourself from it, if you want to succeed in performing or in life.

The comparison with others and the thirst to be the best is also of value in the stage before the performances begin and before the matches start. It is a value that I'm not saying should be deleted from our lives. We are inspired by the success of others and most of us have a thought process that tells us if he or she can do it, so can I. During the course of a performance situation or a match, however, the best results rely on there being no focus on other people. Only after the end of the performance or the match can we welcome back the rather more primitive automatic focus on comparisons. And this can be done with as much enthusiasm as you like – punch the air and shout out to the world: "I'm the best!" A joyous declaration of this kind has nothing to do with how focused the work or the performance has been so far.

But when you are working towards your goal or in the middle of performing, comparisons with others, anxieties about being worse than others, or the desire to be better than others have no value. Focus on anything other than what is going on *now* has no positive impact. At this moment, what is required is a focus on what has to be done, not on anything else or anyone else.

Once this choice has been made and the victory is yours, you are free, on an emotional and almost animalistic level, to embrace the honour, the pride and even the schadenfreude if that is what makes you feel good. Now you are free to revel in the joy of having become the best or achieved what you wanted. But save it until your achievement has been secured and the success is yours.

What you need to do is learn to *choose* when to enter a state of controlled focus, free from the desire to be the best, in the sense of being better than others. Learn to switch from automatic focus to controlled and back again. See the focus model:

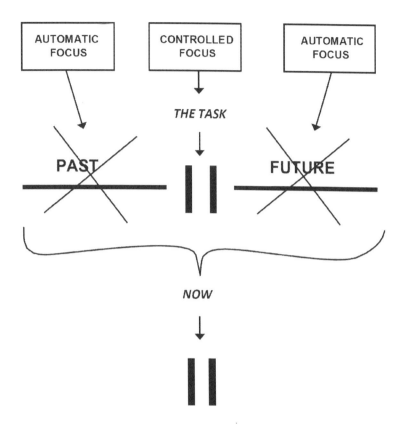

If there is any time in life when our own controlled focus is important, it is when we are choosing what in life we are going to focus on. We should by all means be inspired by what others do, succeed in and win, but when we are making our major league choices, it is preferable to have a conscious focus rooted in our inner core. We should not be governed by the drive to be better than others, or by the desire to outcompete someone. If we can make such a focused choice, it is then easier to maintain a focus on that choice, no matter how slow the progress may be. It becomes easier to avoid being driven by what we think other people believe to be right.

The winners' podium gives a rough indication of who is better than the others. It is therefore unavoidably cool to stand at the very top. Even if you are the best within a relatively narrow discipline, such as shooting, it is still a crystal clear statement that you are the best at something, possibly in the whole world. Getting closer than that to a definition of the word "best" is difficult.

I have stood on a world championship podium a number of times. The first time it happened, I encountered an unexpected emotion.

In the final, I had managed to guide myself from an unfocused state to a state of sharp focus, scored 10.9 with my last shot and secured my first major international medal. I was now seen as "one of them" and it was soon my turn to step forward and climb up onto the podium. I had butterflies in my stomach when the turn came for my discipline and the loudspeakers would soon be calling out my name as "world champion". I had visualised and fantasised about this occasion so many times. During the match, I had managed to keep my thoughts under control and banish the image of the podium from my mind. But now I was free to revel in the eagerly awaited success and drink in all the glory that a person standing at the top of a winners' podium should feel.

I bounded up to the top of the podium. In order not to disappoint anyone in the Swedish Armed Forces, I stood to attention as I waited for my medal. Standing to attention involves bringing the left foot firmly in towards the right, striking your heel into the ground (in this case the podium) with a jerk. I may have been a little over-enthusiastic this time, putting the weight of all that pride into stamping my foot down. As I brought my heel down, straightened my back and stared out across the audience with a proud look, a board that had been sloppily nailed to the front of the podium just in front of my feet fell off – and with it went the big number 1.

The medal presentation, the national anthem and the fanfare continued as usual, but for me the comedy of the moment took the edge off the formality of this otherwise rather pompous ceremony.

Standing as a world champion on a podium whose vital parts are falling off is a paradox worth lingering on. It paints a picture that is at odds with the grand visualisation I, and many like me, have of standing on a winners' podium. Initially, I too thought a new glow would envelop me after having climbed up onto this podium. But as the loose board fell away, I was struck by the pleasing insight that nothing had really changed. I was just the same now as I was before. This was surprisingly good news. It would lend a new calm to the focus on whatever came next, and told me that neither losing nor winning would erase who I *am* at heart.

Here I stand, a medal around my neck, looking out at a beautifully colourful Switzerland and a crowd of applauding spectators, each with their own dreams and desires. I'm pleased, happy, but not euphoric as expected. The world championship podium brings no more positive, life-affirming energy than I felt when I completed the 60-metre dash at school in Ljungby as the mini Hulk, ate egg sandwiches with my mother at the range in Morup or gave a speech in Brussels. It is all the same.

Here I stand, little old me, as a symbol of success, with my number 1 gone. Even a podium has its weaknesses, but what does it matter when the true and lasting value in life can't be found anywhere except deep inside ourselves.

I spare a thought for my old motto: *In my case the push for gold is not only about striving for a medal around my neck, but also about striving for personal development*, and I realise that my development has come not through hours and hours of training, but through a growing insight into the value of maintaining a focus on who I am and not on what I want to be or what I never was. The focus that just helped me to coolly win a gold medal is the same focus that makes me humbly see the wonder of life both on and off the podium. It is the epitome of lifelong learning, and this world championship title and this moment on the podium are just a small step on the path I have chosen to walk through life.

Amongst all this autumn colour, I see myself from high above, standing on a podium, and I can't help but recall the words that an astronaut once uttered when he first looked back at Earth from space:

A fragile bubble of life afloat on a sea of nothing.

In this little bubble, everyone strives for success, happiness and improvement, each on their own path, each in their own way, without finding much time to reflect on the riches of life just as it is.

With just a touch more focus on this truth, wouldn't all our efforts, not to mention life itself, take on even greater meaning?

Start Reclaiming Your Focus!

In today's attention-overloaded society, focus is an especially essential, yet a seldom practiced, skill. Imagine what could be accomplished if you were free to concentrate on the task at hand, fully present and free of distractions.

Christina Bengtsson's philosophy offer insightful advice on how organizations and individuals can achieve their maximum potential and a sustainable living by adopting a focus mindset. From increased quality of work to reduced stress levels, developing this skill has a host of positive effects on one's life.

World champion precision shooter and focus authority, Christina's journey, and the wisdom she's gained along the way, have inspired many around the globe. Today, she lectures and speaks to audiences worldwide, from TEDx stages to international Business Schools and major corporations, and share tools for tapping into our deepest core values, such as her focus model, which can help us thrive in our attention economy.

Christina claims that focus, this vital skill, needs to be given more dedication, both within our self and in all of society.

Christina's mission is to highlight this central societal issue of today and aims to help individuals and organisations to regain lost focus and thereby contribute to a healthy and sustainable society.

As a purchaser of this book, you've made a first step in reclaiming your focus. Continue your progress by visiting Christina's website. www.christinabengtsson.com

Printed in Great Britain
by Amazon

69731060R00097